IMAGES AND WORDS

IMAGES AND WORDS

Change and Chaos in American Culture

Ioannis Stavrianos

Montréal/New York
London

Copyright © 2000 BLACK ROSE BOOKS

No part of this book may be reproduced or transmitted in any form, by any means electronic or mechanical including photocopying and recording, or by any information storage or retrieval system—without written permission from the publisher, or, in the case of photocopying or other reprographic copying, a license from the Canadian Reprography Collective, with the exception of brief passages quoted by a reviewer in a newspaper or magazine.

Black Rose Books No. CC281
Hardcover ISBN: 1-55164-151-8 (bound)
Paperback ISBN: 1-55164-150-X (pbk.)

Canadian Cataloguing in Publication Data
Stavrianos, Ioannis K.
Images and words : change and chaos in american culure

Includes bibliographical references and index.
Hardcover ISBN: 1-55164-151-8 (bound)
Paperback ISBN: 1-55164-150-X (pbk.)

1. Arts and society--United States--History--19th century.
2. Arts, Modern--19th century—United States. I. Title.

NX180.S6S73 1999   700'.973'09034   C99-900474-3

BLACK ROSE BOOKS

C.P. 1258	2250 Military Road	99 Wallis Road
Succ. Place du Parc	Tonawanda, NY	London, E9 5LN
Montréal, H2W 2R3	14150	England
Canada	USA	UK

To order books in North America:
(phone) 1-800-565-9523 (fax) 1-800-221-9985
In Europe: (phone) 0181-986-4854 (fax) 0181-533-5821

Our Web Site address: http://www.web.net/blackrosebooks

A publication of the Institute of Policy Alternatives of Montréal (IPAM)
Printed in Canada

The Canada Council for the Arts
Le Conseil des Arts du Canada

Contents

Acknowledgments..i

Introduction..ix

Chapter One..1
>Ideology and Gender: Lange's *Migrant Mother* and *Drought Victims from Oklahoma*

Chapter Two..35
>The Unconscious and Grotesque Aspect of Walt Whitman's *The Sleepers*

Chapter Three..55
>Variations on the Locomotive and Landscape In George Inness' *Delaware Water Gap* and *Lackawanna Valley*

Chapter Four..115
>Relational Chaos and Residue: Wallace Stevens' *Madame la Fleurie*

Acknowledgments

Since this book includes a collection of essays which have been written over a long period of time, I cannot help but thank all of those people who have influenced me along the way.

I am forever obliged to: Paisley Livingston, William Schultz, Ted Sampson, Robert Crist, Anne Cacoullou, Constantine Evangelides, Peter Ohlin, Peter Gibian, Scott MacKenzie, Liana Sakelliou-Schultz, Sophie Marmaridou, Bessie Dendrinou, and Spyros Iliopoulos.

I am indebted to Dimitri Roussopoulos for his support and timely advice. I would also like to thank Linda Barton for her patience and very fine editing.

On a more personal note, I dedicate this book to my parents, Catherine and Constantine, who have taught me most of what I know and have been with me every step of the way.

Finally, I want to thank Stella for her encouragement, understanding, and love.

To my parents, Catherine and Constantine.

Introduction

"What is the aim of an introduction?" is a question that is all too often passed over in most introductions to a series of collected essays. It is, however, a crucial question that requires an answer—especially in relation to a set of essays. The aims of this introduction are to introduce four essays that have been written in the last decade (1990-1998) and to present some ideas on the possible role of literary criticism. The four essays that will follow are: Ideology and Gender: *Migrant Mother* and *Drought Victims from Oklahoma*; The Unconscious and Grotesque Aspect of Walt Whitman's *The Sleepers*; Variations on the Locomotive and Landscape in George Inness's *Delaware Water Gap* and *The Lackawanna Valley*; and Relational-Chaos and Residue: Wallace Stevens' *Madame la Fleurie*. Part of the function of this introduction will also be to reveal the common threads running through the seemingly unrelated essays. In relation to the second aim of the introduction, an attempt will be made to study Gerald Graff's analytic work on the political consequences of literary criticism and Howard Sankey's views on scientific realism.

It is of critical value to approach the following essays with this question in mind: Are they of any academic or social use? That is, are they meaningful contributions to academic and specific social contexts, or are they simply abstract, dislocated, and therefore unimportant paradigms of discourse. In relation to social relevance the essays that will follow are best placed in this order: 1) Ideology and Gender; 2) The Unconscious and Grotesque Aspect; 3) Relational-Chaos and Residue; and 4) Variations on the Locomotive and Landscape.[1]

Academically, however, the essays follow a different order because of an emphasis on original contribution to scholarship as opposed to social significance and correspondence. The academic order is 3, 1, 4, 2; although, the last two essays (4, 2) fall more or less within the same category or level of importance. Why these essays are placed in the order they appear on the dual hierarchical ladders will be answered shortly, for now it is necessary to answer the question: What is, or are, the primary goals of the essays, and is there a common thread that binds them together?

All of the essays have as their main goal the attempt to reveal the linguistic, artistic,[2] or photographic conventions that are used to convey certain underlying ideas about the real world.[3] Further common threads running through the essays are that they all deal with something American whether it be in photography, poetry, or painting, and all the essays involve textual analyses, one or two objects of study are analyzed in detail.[4]

So far we have examined the common ground on which the essays rest, but what about the differences between them? Without ambivalence the overwhelming difference existing through the four essays has to do with methodology, with the way the objects of analysis are approached. From the earliest essay (Ideology and Gender) to the second and third (The Unconscious and Grotesque Aspect and Variations) to the fourth (Relation-Chaos and Residue) it is clearly noticeable that a triangular methodological shift has transpired: the essays have transferred from a Marxist-feminist perspective to a psychoanalytic and finally to a scientific realist approach, without ever losing focus of the social picture. One may wonder how it is possible for a single author to switch to three radically different approaches within a single work. The response can already be inferred: the essays have been written over a long period of time and indeed reveal progress and the many theoretical interests of the author. The fact of change will also be apparent in relation to writing style and tone: the communication skills have improved by the time one reaches the latter essays, and the tone of voice of the fourth essay is almost foreign to the voice in the previous essays.

An analysis of the strengths and weaknesses of each essay in relation to social and academic relevance will now follow. The first essay, Ideology and Gender was written in 1991. Before examining anything further, it is best to introduce the essay by asking and then answering the question: What is it about? Ideology and Gender is, very simply, concerned with the in-depth analysis, from a Marxist-feminist framework, of two of Dorothea Lange's RA/FSA (1930s) photographs. One of the two photographs is well known (*Migrant Mother*), whereas the other one (*Drought Victims from Oklahoma*) is a photograph of constructed oppression which has surprisingly received little popular or academic attention.

The objective of Ideology and Gender is to reveal the ways in which female oppression in the 1930s context of America was, amongst other means, constructed through seemingly innocent photographs of women and their families. Now that the essay has been introduced, a review of its strengths and weaknesses is in order.

As far as weaknesses are concerned, there are at least three substandard elements in Ideology and Gender: one, the theoretical material used to study the topic is dated;

two, the topic (female oppression in Dorothea Lange's photography) has not been researched enough; and three, the communicative skills are still immature. On the other hand, the strength of the essay is its argument. Is this enough to make it a useful essay? The answer is positive only because all arguments attempting to reveal the mechanisms of social oppression, whether in relation to women, blacks, or other minorities, have to be presented repeatedly because oppressive modes, practices, and functions are still in evidence in our modern ideological structures.[6]

One may, however, wonder if it is of any contemporary social relevance to examine the constructive processes involved in the "cause/effect" ideological structures of the 1930s in America. The answer is once again affirmative: it is of equal importance to study historical and present causes of oppression because the former types of analyses could teach us how not to accept, uncritically, previously used ideological patterns and methods. In sum, Ideology and Gender is an essay of extreme social relevance since what it describes actually corresponds to actual social practices, but it is slightly less important academically even though it does contribute to the theory of the sometimes suspicious and exploitative interdependence of photography and reality.[7]

The essay The Unconscious and Grotesque Aspect of Walt Whitman's *The Sleepers* was written in 1992, a year after Ideology and Gender. It is a psychoanalytic reading of a specific part (about ten pages) of Whitman's *Leaves of Grass*. More specifically, the essay is an attempt to interpret *The Sleepers* within the constraints of dream. In other words, *The Sleepers* is reduced to being a dream in writing that is open to a variety of unconscious based analyses. It is further argued that as a dream it reveals content—as all dreams do according to Freud—that is normally repressed. The content of the dream is of interest in connection to both Whitman and the more general context of nineteenth century America. (Throughout *The Sleepers* Whitman has created such a perfect synthesis of the personal and the communal that, at times, it is difficult to distinguish between the two.)

In relation to the collective unconscious of nineteenth century America—and the sleeper-persona (Whitman) does play the role of representative and speaker of the nation[8]—the dream points to high levels of conscious repression and the potential eruption of such restraint. The aspects of collective conscious experience that suffer surplus repression and are therefore expressed uncontrollably in the dream are: violence; homoeroticism; death; the binary opposites: fragmentation and unity; and military defeat. What is of social significance here is the interdependent concept of surplus repression and eruption, of the idea that if something is repressed too much or too long, it will eventually (erupt) seek expression in dreams, and even potentially in conscious life in the forms of neurosis and psychosis at the individual level, and aggression at the collective level.

In many ways, then, Whitman's *The Sleepers* is a telling example of the effects repressive ideological models can produce in the collective and individual sphere. And it is clear that American culture and politics has much to learn from studying such patterns of behaviour—in order to avoid them in the future—as are witnessed in the real American setting and in the sublime poetic fragments of *The Sleepers*.

The Unconscious and Grotesque Aspect is a generally strong essay, and is socially relevant since it describes a "cause/effect" paradigm that applies to real social settings but is less important academically because the topic is not researched well enough and a socio-historical instead of a psychoanalytic base—in which what was actually transpiring in nineteenth century America is directly applied to the dream—would have permitted for a more concrete and less creative treatment of the issues.

The third essay, Variations on the Locomotive and Landscape in George Inness's *Delaware Water Gap* and *The Lackawanna Valley* was written in 1993. Once again the topic is nineteenth century American society, only this time it is examined through two of George Inness' paintings and the philosophical work of Ralph Waldo Emerson. The general approach of Variations, as the title suggests, is to apply an eclectic theoretical base—grounded in psychoanalysis (object-relations and Freudian theory), socio-historical analysis, and semiotic theory—to *Delaware Water Gap*, an idyllic pastoral representation, and *The Lackawanna Valley*, a more complex and "realistic"[9] painting, in an attempt to reveal how social and technological change and determination are handled in mid-nineteenth century American Art. The essay is, therefore, concerned with the sometimes transparent correspondence between philosophy, art, society, and technology. The objects of study in Variations exhibit clearly the ways in which the collective culture of the period is coping with the appearance of the locomotive in the landscape.

Interestingly enough, in Variations, unlike Ideology and Gender, the representational objects seem to be both affected by, and affective of, reality. That is, they are (because of their transitional history) simultaneously determined by what is taking place in the social context and are determining factors of that context.[10] The paintings are, therefore, paradoxically conscious and unconscious artefacts of what transpired in mid-nineteenth century America.

In respect to social and academic relevance the essay under scrutiny placed fourth and third under the above categories. This does not mean that Variations is not worth reading, it is after all one of the better written essays, but it does have some glaring weaknesses. Academically, it does not offer an original contribution to scholarship, even though the topic is well researched, since the primary aim of the essay is "creative game playing." Furthermore, although Variations states a thesis about the social and artistic world, it does not offer a concrete model of potential social action or behaviour, and thus it remains, for the most part, a purely experimental academic essay.

The final essay, Relational Chaos and Residue: Wallace Stevens' *Madame la Fleurie,* was written in 1997, several years after the previous essays. Like Ideology and Gender it studies expression in the American twentieth century. But it is also connected to the other two essays in this book, because Wallace Stevens' mode of expression, like Whitman's and Emerson's, falls under the literary category of transcendentalism.[11] The basic focus of Relational Chaos and Residue is the analytic study of a specific type of indeterminacy (relational-chaotic) in Stevens' *Madame La Fleurie*. Relational Chaos and Residue is a fascinating, but difficult contribution to the analysis of indeterminate structure in Stevens' poetry. The primary aim of the essay is to probe the causes and effects of indeterminacy in *Madame La Fleurie*, while the secondary, but nevertheless crucial interest is to present the idea that indeterminacy in Stevens' poetry is consciously constructed, and not an accident that is arrived at by chance.

Of further relevance to the essay is the concept of realism, and whether Stevens' poetry qualifies as realistic (as he would often have it) or not. Thus, if Stevens' poetry is considered realistic, a necessary consequence of such a statement is that the world is governed, solely, by chaotic and disorderly principles since most of Stevens' verse is involved in the construction of chaotic and disorderly structures of communication. This argument, however, is criticized heavily as lacking a rigorous enough connection to the real world. Reality, it is argued, cannot be reduced to fragmentation, disorder, or chaos; a more analytic account of the objective world would have to describe at the very least some form of synthesis: some events are disorderly, whereas others are not. Moreover there could be another sense of synthesis prevailing in some forms of experience in which both disorderly and orderly physical structures are at work simultaneously. A consequence of Stevens' reductive understanding of reality is that at no point can his poetry function well within the constraints of realism.

In relation to the academic and social ladder of relevance, Relational Chaos and Residue is considered the most important essay for the former category, but it does not do as well for the latter one. It is without doubt one of the more analytic accounts of indeterminacy in Stevens that one can find in the academic field: the topic is extensively researched, and several original theses are presented. Its strong point, however, is also its weak point when placed within the context of social significance: although Relational Chaos and Residue offers much insight on the physical world, it does not advance any concrete comments on issues pertaining to the world of social interaction.

Now that the essays have been contextualized, it is worth examining one of the potential roles of literary criticism. All forms of criticism, according to the present belief of the author, should work toward the ideals of truth and progress. Why? one might counter, and further ask, at the expense of which other approach? The response to both questions is: if literary criticism does not strive toward truth and progress then it will continue to exist at the periphery of modern discursive practices that have a direct effect on the way the social world functions; and the alternative to analytic modes of inquiry are modes concerned with artistic creation. All of this is not to say that the end result of art in literary criticism is unacceptable, this would be a foolish argument to make, but we are living in a world in which the paradigms of knowledge are not based in literary or critical inquiry anymore, and it would seem that the latter at least, literary criticism, should in some way be oriented toward social contribution.

The only recourse out of the periphery of modern discourse would certainly involve a redirection of emphasis toward the possibility of arriving at truth and progress, of honesty, and high levels of research instead of pure creativity and obscurity in literary criticism. A common step in this direction would inevitably mean that literary criticism, like scientific modes of discourse, would at least be read and thought about in relation to what it can offer the practical world. On the other hand, if literary criticism is simply obsessed with artistic and obscurantist modes of discourse, then there is no reason (apart from pleasure) to be writing it, since it could never affect the social world.

Let us now focus on a more specific list of the possible roles for literary criticism:

1. Examine, as a critic, the specific works of an author in detail. Always prefer close textual analyses of a few representative poems than superficial, all encompassing analyses. Inquiries into the complete work of an author are hardly ever possible (there is just too much work of sometimes unrelated variety to consider), but in those cases where a critic attempts to do so (and there are many examples), the final result is all too often a general discourse that cannot illustrate the actual patterns and structures of the texts he or she chooses to interpret.

2. Analytic and consciousness grounded critical approaches to literature, photography, art, etc., are preferable to unconscious and artistic based models. Consciousness in all its forms, including the way it

may manifest itself in poetry, is all that we, as critics, have to study empirically. And since consciousness is still a mystery—most scientists agree upon this—criticism should try to explain parts of its complex structure, analytically, in a collective attempt to reach a fuller understanding of everyday experience in the future. It is only once more knowledge of conscious experience is gained that we may then turn our attention to studying analytically, unconscious experience (if indeed such a mode exists at all).

3. If it is possible, approaches to literature should relate directly or indirectly to a real world. That is, whenever it is possible to do so, literary criticism should create a correspondence relation between the interpretation of the text of study and the world outside it. The basic ideal here is to achieve concrete instead of abstract modes of criticism.

4. Interdisciplinary approaches to texts are of value, especially when the critic knows well the adjacent field or fields he or she is working with. Theoretical models from the fields of science, philosophy, anthropology, sociology, psychology, politics, and economics can contextualize and shed necessary light on the objects of literature, poetry, photography, theatre, cinema, and art. All too often, however, critics use models from other fields of knowledge without enough rigour, without knowing the supporting field well enough.[12] Doing so is just as bad as not using an interdisciplinary approach.

5. The objective of truth in criticism (whether in relation to coherence, correspondence, or pragmatism) and the study of the nature of literary and artistic objects is necessary. Truth in criticism implies the use of reason and evidence in critical inquiry. A common effort in this methodological direction will eventually mean that

as a field of knowledge, literary criticism will be more logically oriented than it is today. A more logical discourse that is in some manner connected to the facts of the world is synonymous with more respect, power, and social relevance for literary criticism. Furthermore, an emphasis on studying the nature (the structures and conventions) of literary and artistic objects is imperative in order for overall progress to be achieved in literary criticism.[13]

6. Because literary criticism can, potentially, influence a real world if it is taken seriously enough, an author must be conscious of the potential political consequences of his or her work, but this never at the expense of rational, truth based inquiry. In other words, first comes the objective of rationality in literary research, and then follows the very important objective of political consequence.[14]

7. Finally, a critic should never lose sight of the ideals of equality, tolerance, and understanding in his or her discipline. It is of primary importance that all discourses and objects of study are open to debate and analysis.

Notes

1. From this point onward shorter forms of the titles will appear.

2. "Artistic" is specifically used to describe paintings in this context.

3. There is an especially strong correspondence between the underlying sense(s) of the objects of study and the real world. In many ways, the photographs in Ideology and Gender and the paintings in Variations function, respectively, within the "cause/effect" paradigms of propaganda and advertisement.

4. These two common links seem to reveal strongly the fact that "one mind" wrote the essays.

5. "Triangular" is used creatively to signify triadic.

6. For a persuasive argument on modern ideological practices see Gerald Graff's "The Pseudo-Politics of Interpretation," in *Critical Inquiry*, 9 March (1983), p. 607.

7. On the suspicious otherness of photography see Walter Benjamin's and Roland Barthes' work on the subject.

8. The sleeper-persona in *The Sleepers* is a literary example of the grotesque body, of a body that represents and unites everything (subjects and objects). See Michail Bakhtin's *Rabelais and His World*, trans. Hélène Iswolsky (Bloomington: Indiana University Press, 1984), p. 26—27, for an inspired definition of the grotesque body.

9. "Realistic" is used here in the sense of conveying the actual collective outlook or sentiment of the time. Otherwise, the form of *The Lackawanna Valley* is similar to that of *Delaware Water Gap*.

10. I am clearly making reference here to Cornelius Castoriadis's theory of social practice, which involves both a created and creative element.

11. Harold Bloom was the first to popularize the idea that Whitman and Emerson were Stevens' true precursors.

12. See Gerald Graff for a convincing argument on the importance of knowing well the disciplines with which one chooses to examine literature, "The Pseudo-Politics of Interpretation," in *Critical Inquiry*, 9 March (1983), p. 608.

13. See Howard Sankey's "Hilary Putnam's Internal Realism," in *Cogito* 12:1 (1998), p. 33—34, for an enlightening discussion on truth, progress, and scientific realism.

14. Graff insists, in the afore mentioned essay, that politics and power are irrelevant to a theory's truth value. This is unquestionably correct, but it is seems that a critic can still try to alter the potential political outcome of a theory while always keeping in sight the goal of truth.

Ideology and Gender:
Lange's *Migrant Mother*
and
Drought Victims From Oklahoma

1

> Nature must be expressed in symbols; nature is known through symbols which are themselves a construction upon experience, a product of mind, an artifice or conventional product, therefore the reverse of natural.
>
> —Mary Douglas, *Natural Symbols*

> Images have become our true sex object, the object of our desire...It is this promiscuity and the ubiquity of images, this viral contamination of things by images which are the fatal characteristics of our culture. And this knows no bounds, because...images cannot be prevented from proliferating indefinitely.
>
> —Jean Baudrillard, *The Ecstasy Of Communication*

Despite the failure of this essay to carry out significant research, it still has an important thesis to present. The thesis is: at one level, Dorothea Lange's most popular photographs systemically construct an oppressive narrative for women; at another level, however, they allow room for an interpretation of Women's contradictory and impossible role in patriarchy. To read Lange's photographs as Wendy Kozol does in "Madonnas of the Fields: Photography, Gender, and 1930s Farm Relief" as statements which reinforce the dominant ideology of the 1930s in America is indeed correct. After all, such an approach sheds historical and political light on Lange's photography. But to remain within a singularly strict "photography equals dominant ideology" framework misses the point. Lange's photography is not always an example of simple ideological documentation. *Migrant Mother* and *Drought Victims from Oklahoma*, for instance, reveal a true tension between woman and her role as it is described in patriarchal ideology. It is therefore necessary to suggest that within Lange's documents of dominant New Deal ideology hints of subversion surface; blindspots and weaknesses seem to appear in the ideological structures.

The following question must then be asked: where does one locate the subversive quality in the dominant ideological structures of *Migrant Mother* and *Drought Victims from Oklahoma*? The answer is simple: in the field of vision. In *Drought Victims from Oklahoma*, her field of vision is very different from his. Is this difference in the sphere of vision an example of the possibility that a separate space—one outside patriarchy—exists for women? More importantly: does not this difference in vision—this looking elsewhere—point to women's contradictory and impossible existence in patriarchy? With Tania Modleski's help an answer to these questions will be supplied at a later stage in the essay. For now, it will suffice to introduce the constructions in Lange's photography that oppose vehemently any kind of subversion where women are concerned.

Lange is very consistent in her representation of women. 'Woman'[1] is often a mother, sometimes a wife, and always an abstraction. That is, the 'woman' in Lange's photography eternally escapes her material circumstances. A strong example of such an escape from material conditions is to be found in *Wife of a Migrant Labourer*. The wife becomes little more than a symbol of tragedy. The conditions that have led her to adopt a tragic pose evidently exist outside the photograph and are, it would seem, of little relevance to the ideological narrative. Lange has constructed a "Tragic Woman," through gesture and facial expression, that is in no way a liberating or positive example for women in the real world. But the key question to ask here is whether any relation exists between the tragic construction of woman in some of Lange's photographs and the dominant socio-political climate of the 1930s. The answer is positive, a relation most certainly exists.

New Deal conservative ideology of the 1930s determined the need for tragic representations of woman. Tragic woman (that most vulnerable creature in patriarchal society) alone would secure sympathy, support, and aid in a period of hardship for her victimized agricultural companions. Similarly, ideological structures of the 1930s determined the need to represent woman as either wife or mother/keeper of the family. In the context of a failing economy, the state felt one institution had to remain strong: the family. Who was to bear the burden of the family? Both of Lange's photographs quite simply provide the answer: Woman. Moreover, 1930s conservative ideology also determined the lack of sexuality and femininity that would appear in Lange's photography.

The theoretical framework and methodology that will be used to examine Lange's *Drought Victims* and *Migrant Mother* will here be presented. The initial stages of the essay will explore Louis Althusser's definition of ideology. Then more conventional definitions and theories of ideology and hegemony will be explored. Once the ideology/hegemony framework is completed, a variety of feminist criticism and theory on the cultural construction of gender identity will be analysed. After the theoretical section of the essay is completed, a textual reading of *Drought Victims from Oklahoma*,

Migrant Mother and *Wife of a Migrant Labourer* will follow. The method of analysis will be simple: each photograph will be isolated, described, and examined in relation to the theoretical framework of the previous pages. Most of the theory will be taken from Janet Todd's *Feminist Literary History*, Rosemarie Tong's *Feminist Thought*, Tania Modleski's *The Women Who Knew Too Much: Hitchcock and Feminist Theory*, Mary Daly's *Beyond God the Father: Toward a Philosophy of Women's Liberation*, Wendy Kozol's "Madonnas of the Fields: Photography, Gender, and 1930s Farm Relief" and Michel Foucault's *The History of Sexuality: Volume 1*.

Finally, since this is an essay which will explore and examine the manner in which women's oppression is naturalized in the cultural construction of gender identity, the stand point of the essay must be made clear. For the most part Lange's photographs will be approached from a Marxist-feminist position which will always keep in focus the existence of other forms of feminist discourse. There will be a consistent return to the idea that women's material oppression is real and that one cannot correct such a grave injustice through the artificial and symbolic construction of woman.

Ideology And Hegemony

For Jacques Lacan, men and women are born in language. In the essay "Ideology and Ideological state Apparatuses," Louis Althusser argues instead that men and women are born into an ideological framework. Ideology, for Althusser, is a material reality that functions largely as an "unreflected condition of acting and existing within a commonplace world."[2] Ideological structures, therefore, take hold of a subject's unconscious. Ideology, according to Althusser, does not function at the level of a set of conscious and voluntary ideas. Consequently, individual historical subjects do not choose their ideology or initiate it. In essence, then, ideology does not set itself up as being consciously chosen, but instead appears in the forms of nationality or nature, as something unquestionable and given. Althusser concisely describes ideology as "that system of beliefs and assumptions—unconscious, unexamined, invisible—which represent the imaginary relationship of individuals to their real conditions of existence."[3] Similar to Lacan's theory of the subject's role in language and society, Althusser's definition of ideology takes for granted that subjects perform fictional narratives.

A shift from a definition of ideology which lays heavy emphasis on unconscious absorption, as does Althusser's, to a more conventional and conscious based definition is now worth looking at. Unlike Althusser, Roland Barthes took ideology to mean "any knowledge that is posed as natural or generally applicable,"[4] especially when its social origins are suppressed or considered irrelevant. Thus, in *Mythologies*, wine comes to stand as a national signifier of French substance, strength, and unity. The material reality of the production of wine, however, is that the people who produce it in Algeria remain oppressed. Ideology is, then, a form of abstract, unrelated, and false thought. No strong connection necessarily exists between the idea and the material conditions and relationships that are part of a product or event. As part of a social system ideology, therefore, has the capacity to produce and reproduce continuously abstract social relations of inequality. But where are these social relations of inequality produced?

Both Raymond Williams and Roland Barthes agree on this point: within the sphere of signification and discourse.[5] Both thinkers also agree that ideology runs parallel with the ruling class of a society. The ways of making sense of the world are continually being produced and distributed, for the most part, by those classes which hold power. The distribution of ruling class ideology is, however, much more universal. That is, it is indeed possible for people outside the ruling classes, such as Dorothea Lange and even street-corner ambassadors, to distribute ideology. This fact is the true revelation of the monumental strength of a dominant ideology: it invades all areas of society. John Fiske summarizes the function of ideology in society in *Key Concepts in Communication*:

> This ideology is the means by which ruling economic classes generalize and extend their supremacy across the whole range of social activity, and naturalize it in the process, so that their rule is accepted as natural and inevitable, and erefore legitimate and binding.[6]

Of relevance to the discussion is the notion that if we retain ideology but find substitutes for class structure, such as gender and race, for example, the categories of male ideology and white ideology begin to surface. They are as much part of the ideological realm as ruling class ideology is. The hegemonic process operates, as Fiske describes it, "in the realm of consciousness and representation."[7]

Hegemony will be taken to mean the process whereby men's and women's consent "is actively sought for in those ways of making sense of the world which happen to fit in with the interests of the hegemonic alliance of classes, or (the) power bloc."[8] In other words, hegemony is a naturalization of what is, historically, a class ideology. Hegemony is the ruling class' ability to render its philosophy, structure of life as common sense. Propaganda is the efficient cultural mode of representation which attempts to render the hegemonic process possible by intentionally promoting a certain party or class ideology. (Although it is not clear whether Dorothea Lange's photography is propaganda, it does, to be sure, promote Roosevelt's New Deal ideology.⁹) Propaganda is, therefore, closely tied to hegemony. Its function is (and this will reveal itself to some degree in Lange's photography) to intentionally manipulate images so that they will favor a dominant power bloc.

More must be said about the types of institutions the hegemonic process relies upon, and whether women take part in these institutions. According to Fiske, the great producers and distributors of hegemony are the State, the law, the media and the family. These institutions are eternal producers of sense and knowledge—they are cultural institutions whose role is to produce individual and social consciousness.¹⁰ They are the very institutions that produce the man/woman distinction, and the master/slave construction. The state is in many ways the father of hegemonic process; it is from the state that information is channelled through to the other institutions. (This is particularly true for the 1930s. The state as father of the hegemonic process was no longer an accepted idea by the 1970s.) It is easy to see this process at work when one realizes that Roosevelt's political agenda came first in the 1930s and Lange's photography, which is an expression of Roosevelt's politics in the media realm, came second.

This is to say that the hegemonic process—the conditioning process of men and women in the 1930s—was essentially male; that is, the power bloc (State and legal system) was primarily composed of men who had the power to produce and distribute ideology which would serve their purposes. Lange's contribution to the production of New Deal ideology was evident. She was very much part of the hegemonic process for the simple reason that she worked within a medium (photography) which was often given strict notions of what to produce. The strong narrative of what the institution of the family should be was continually being produced and reproduced in

Lange's photography. It is fair to claim, then, that her portrayal of the family was greatly determined by New Deal ideology of the 1930s. Consequently, it is necessary to reveal the way Lange's photographic repertoire works within the ideology/hegemony framework of the period. Hegemonic structure, according to Wendy Kozol, was consciously produced in Lange's photograhy. But, even if it was not consciously produced, Althusser's definition of ideology permits one to argue that a text, in this case Lange's photography, and the ideological context inevitably and unconsciously converge. This condition allows one to examine the ideological/hegemonic structures in the photographs irrespective of whether they were consciously or unconsciously reproduced.

The Cultural Construction Of Gender Identity

Ideology is precisely what gives shape to culture. What is understood to be culture in a given society is nothing more than a set of ideological codes brought together in perfect unity. The invisible but nevertheless material structure of a cultural is, therefore, produced through ideological construction. It is within such a theoretical framework that the concept of gender—of the cultural differentiation of male from female—should be placed.

In the final chapter of *Sexual Politics*, Kate Millet argues that difference and inequality between the sexes is culturally constructed. According to Millet, gender is a psychological concept referring to cultural identity. Difference in the sexes is not a natural given as women have been tricked into thinking: Millet illustrates how frighteningly easy gender identity is to lose in her interesting analysis of Jean Genet's homosexual novels and plays. Gender identity, or the cultural construction of the terms masculine and feminine had simply come to encode in Millet's view nothing more than notions of high and low, master and servant, with men always being on the winning end.[11]

Difference for Lacan, and his French feminist disciples, Helene Cixous and Luce Irigaray, is derived through language. Instead of an ideological/cultural construction of gender, Lacan argues that language in itself situates the subject in a gender category. Language, as Lacan points out, exists within the realm of the phallus. It is continually being created and recreated by men who have complete control over it. What is the consequence of language being male? The answer is simple: women cannot exist as subjects. For that reason, Kristeva and Irigaray argue for 'feminine writing' and experimentation in phallic language. Nevertheless, what should be stressed here is that Lacan, like Millet, treats the fact of having a male or female body as irrelevant. For Lacan, division and difference only ever occur within language. Without language, there is neither gender nor gender-oriented desire.[12] It is the particular chain of words that are associated with either man or woman that unconsciously place the subject in one gender or another.

According to Kate Millet and Mary Daly ideology is patriarchal. For Millet, patriarchal ideology is always engaged in the process of exaggerating biological difference between men and women.[13] In doing so it makes certain that men always have the dominant (masculine) roles and that women always have the subordinate (feminine) ones. (The master/slave power relation is very much in evidence in the ideological structure of the 1930s). Patriarchal ideology is so powerful that through modes of conscious conditioning men secure the seeming consent of the very women they oppress.[14] Oppression toward women is naturalized in such male institutions as the academy, the church, and the family.

A crucial question must be asked at this point: what happens to a woman who refuses to accept her role in patriarchy? Millet is quick to answer: if the conditioning process is not completely effective, the next step is intimidation, or as she puts it, coercion.[15]

The goal of patriarchal ideology, then, is to have women internalize a sense of inferiority. Mary Daly's argument against patriarchy follows in the same steps as Millet's. In *Beyond God the Father*, Daly observes that femininity and whatever it comes to connote is constructed under patriarchy. Daly does, however, take Millet's argument a step further: not only is gender a male cultural construction, but also under the construction models of patriarchal ideology are female sexuality and reproduction. Nothing escapes the patriarchal machinery, to the point where women become nothing more than a man made construct, as Rosemarie Tong observes in her analysis of Daly's work:

> If patriarchy has constructed femininity—if it has constructed Mary and Eve, the madonna and the whore, the positive feminine qualities of nurturance, compassion, and gentleness and the negative feminine qualities of pettiness, jealousy, and vanity—then there is good reason for women to reject everything for which these labels stand.

"Femininity," asserts Daly, "is a man-made construct, having nothing to do with femaleness."[16] In short, male ideology is the material involved in the cultural construction of women.

Women vs. Woman

As I have pointed out, Lange does not escape the ideological current of her time. Nevertheless, it must also be added that a perfect, flawless ideological product is hardly ever possible. Blindspots and weaknesses in even the best propaganda can be detected.[17] In Lange's *Migrant Mother* and *Drought Victims*, the women's gaze reveals weakness in the ideological narrative; it is impossible to control the interpretation of a female gaze that is directed outside our spectatorial field of vision. But even this subversive quality of the photographs is not enough to allow one to argue that they are not cultural creations of gender identity. It bears repeating that woman in *Migrant Mother* and *Drought Victims* is a mother, fixed in her nurturing role. Her specific story, as Kazol argues, is never told.

The Women/Woman distinction is a crucial one for Janet Todd. 'Her' story as opposed to *his*tory must some day be expressed if women are ever to escape material oppression and socio-cultural constraint. Everywhere in representation, observes Todd, the abstract form of woman is chosen at the expense of the material form of women. To continue representing women as woman is to continue a long tradition of historical oppression. To emphasize women, on the other hand, in literature and photography, is to pay attention to the everyday, concrete details of women's existence in patriarchal society. By paying close attention to women, Todd believes the concreteness of women's oppression will make itself visible. In essence, Todd is advocating a socio-historical materialist approach to women's experience which would reveal oppression throughout the ages. She steers her readers away from French feminist theory because of its tendency towards the creation of a female goddess. As far as Todd is concerned, thinkers like Cixous, Irigaray, and Kristeva remain in the realm of wishful thinking. Todd's approach is in fact simple: all she asks of feminist writing is to pay close attention to both the signifier women and to the material conditions of women's experience. The following quotation from Janet Todd's Feminist Literary History sums up well her argument:

I do not see the need to follow them (the French feminist theorists) into the supplanting of women by woman or women's voices by ungendered writing in the feminine by men and women. Women are, after all, in history as material entities, they are more than mothers, and they form a kind of non-identical paradigm of the historical process itself.[18]

Drought Victims from Oklahoma

The photograph is definitely fraught with narrative signification. It comes to mean so much when placed under an ideological and feminist framework. At first the general details of the photograph will be described; then an examination of its semantic structure will follow.

The father, with a look and gesture of despair, is in the foreground. His field of vision is directed somewhere in the vicinity of the spectators. His hands are dirty and a little bit of stubble is growing on his face. The mother is in the background holding her child in her arms. The visual form of mother and child is similar to that of the Virgin Mary and Christ-child as represented in traditional Christian icons. The mother's field of vision, unlike the father's, is unlocatable. Her vision is directed completely outside the spectators normal sphere of perception. An important question to ask here is: who is looking where? And why is her visual field not the same as his? Can the concept of power be associated with different fields of vision? The responses to these questions will be given shortly. For now, it will suffice to continue the description of the photograph.

It is easy to see that only a tent protects them. The tent replaces the home in their case. A large tree rests in the background. The mother and father are on a raised, flat, wooden structure. In the extreme lower right-hand corner, a foot makes its way into the image, suggesting there are more members in the family. Behind the woman there is a space of whiteness, giving one the impression of infinite space. Anxiety and worry are written all over the mother's face as the child stares down the middle of the photograph. The mother's dress is torn and dirty.

The narrative in *Drought Victims* can be summed up in a few sentences. The father is out of work. The madonna and child, who are always seen as the most vulnerable and helpless in patriarchal society, are in desperate need of help. There is light (whiteness), hope at the end of the tunnel if only we offer to help this destitute family. The RA/FSA mission, as Kazol points out, was to get middle class sympathy and economic support for the farm victims of the 1930s.

The Naturalization Of The Madonna And Child

To begin, let us look at the mother and child relationship in Lange's *Drought Victims*. In LUKE 2:35 the Christ-child is being presented in the temple when the prophet Simeon walks up to the Virgin Mary and tells her the prophecy: Thy son will be a knife in thy heart.[19] The prophecy clearly tells the Virgin mother that her suffering will come as a result of her child. In *Drought Victims* one can almost read the mother as a Virgin Mary. That is, the mother's suffering, like the Virgin Mary's, is of mythical proportion. To be sure, the Virgin Mary suffered greatly for her son. Can a similar fate be predicted for the mother in *Drought Victims*? The mother is the one holding the child in her arms; this could translate to the idea that she is the one who has to bear the burden of holding the family together.

Upon further reflection it is clear that the photograph serves as a prediction of the mother's future suffering. Not only is motherhood naturalized in the photograph, but also the concept that the mother will have to suffer to keep the family together. So it is 'taken for granted' that woman equals mother, and that woman belongs in the institution of the family. To have the mother hold the child in her arms also naturalizes another concept: the nurturing mother. This function is especially true when you find Lange taking a series of photographs during the 1930s in which mothers are represented with their young.

There is unquestionably a profound sexism at work in such mass produced imagery of mother and child. Women in these images are, very simply, confined exclusively to nurturing roles. It is crucial to ask here whether it is natural for women to be mothers? Or whether it is natural for women to suffer, and to exist solely within the family unit? The answer to these questions is negative: a woman does not by necessity have to be a mother, nor does she have to suffer and exist within the constraints of a family. Nevertheless, it was deemed natural and necessary by Franklin Roosevelt and a country in crisis to mafacture a type of woman that could keep the institution of family from falling apart. Consequently, the underlying narrative of *Drought Victims* is: women first reproduce and then they nurture, or mother that which is reproduced. What follows is an illustration representing the structure of the hegemonic naturalization process of woman in *Drought Victims*:

Diagram 1:

Woman in Drought Victims signifies:

  A) Reproduction

  B) Motherhood

  C) Childbearing (Pain and suffering is 'naturalized' in this   part of he construction process.)

  D) The Family

What does feminist theory have to present against such a structure of conditioning? We know that Kate Millet and Mary Daly would dismiss *Drought Victims* as nothing more than patriarchal construction. Daly would especially critize the construction of the 'positive' feminine qualities of the Madonna: namely nurturance, compassion, and gentleness. Millet's chief argument against such representation would be that by fixing woman in the patriarchal institution of the family, 'which justifies and reinforces women's subordination to men,' women are left with an artefact which works in the conditioning of an internalized sense of inferiority. Wendy Kozol and Janet Todd would strongly argue that such a structure of conditioning overlooks women's material reality and possible oppression. From a psychoanalytic feminist perspective, Dorothy Dinnerstein and Nancy Chodorow would find *Drought Victims* a distributing representation indeed. Both would agree that the true oppression of women originates in the female monopoly on mothering. (As has been argued previously, *Drought Victims* firmly positions woman in the role of the mother.) Like all Freudian based critics, Dinnerstein and Chodorow feel the family unit determines society. Hence, the law, politics, economics, and cultural institutions would be radically different if women did not have to think of themselves as mothers.[20]

Field Of Vision In Drought Victims

Let us begin with a simple observation: 'her' field of vision is not the same as 'his.' She is looking in another visual field. A simple deduction can therefore be made: female vision is separate from male vision in *Drought Victims*. It is this difference in field of perception which renders Lange's photograph subversive. This separate field of vision is the mark which is at tension with the systematic and conscious construction process of woman in *Drought Victims.*

Male vision, in *Drought Victims*, is directed somewhere within the vicinity of the spectators' position. There is nothing eccentric about the father's field of vision; it is, in fact, conventional and therefore patriarchal (within the limits of the center). The father's and child's perceptual fields are within the patriarchal sphere. (It is assumed here that the very role of spectatorship, the way we read and 'look' at representation, is determined by patriarchal ideology.) Female (the mother's) vision, on the other hand, is outside the patriarchal sphere and into the sphere of what Kristeva would probably name 'the semiotic' or, possibly into the Lacanian sphere of the 'imaginary.'

An examination of Lacan's distinction between 'the symbolic' and 'the imaginary' is necessary in order to have a foundation from which to understand Julia Kristeva's theory of 'the semiotic space.' For Lacan, language, together with psychological structures, culture and politics, only ever exists within the phallic realm, within the realm of men. Constructed by men, the order of patriarchy is named by Lacan "the symbolic": in this realm both women and men must exist. The symbolic is for Lacan what 'the social' would be for Janet Todd.

In contrast to 'the symbolic' is 'the imaginary.' The imaginary is the pre-oedipal, pre-linguistic realm where there is no separation of self and other or mother and infant. It is the realm which 'feeds into the unconscious and is founded on an illusion of wholeness.'[21] The chaotic realm of 'the imaginary' is therefore in opposition to 'the symbolic.' Although Lacan never did make any connection between women and 'the imaginary,' it is clear to see a positive connection existing between women's experience and the 'other' space of the imaginary. The existence

IDEOLOGY AND GENDER   19

of a relation—between women's normal and potentially subversive experience and the imaginary or semiotic realm is a worthwhile consideration in respect to *Drought Victims*. The woman in *Drought Victims* is clearly living under oppressive circumstances. Is not her gaze into an undefinable sphere a mark of her desire to transcend her present reality of living in the family as a nurturing mother? Within a Lacanian framework, is she not possibly dreaming of an 'imaginary' existence outside 'the symbolic.' It is important to recall that 'the imaginary' is that stage in life which precedes our entrance into the symbolic realm of patriarchy. Is it not fair to say that the mother in *Drought Victims* may just wish a return?

The mother's vision can be interpreted more rigorously within the conceptual bracket of Julia Kristeva's theory of the semiotic space. Women, according to Kristeva, are represented as objects in a world purely determined by the universal phallic signifier. Women could never have power if Lacan's idiom of the symbolic is accepted. So how could a woman escape the Lacanian bind according to Kristeva? She must create and have faith in the concept of 'the semiotic,' which is, at best, only a slight modification of Lacan's 'imaginary.' The semiotic is a space that only women could have access to. It is that space which precedes the symbolic, and is never entirely repressed in it. That is, the semiotic exists somewhere beyond the visible/invisible patterns of patriarchy and is never appropriated into dominant culture. It is, as Janet Todd points out, a separate space and one from which women can disrupt patriarchal language:

> The semiotic space was beyond the subject or the enunciator as traditionally understood and separate from the realm in which political and cultural ideology was inscribed. It was also beyond the passive and conservative imaginary of Lacan and

could function as the locus of disruption, displacing the symbolic order where patriarchal language existed and where the male logos was king.[22]

The disruption of patriarchal language could bring about a social shift, as Todd observes. The symbolic (the domain of male power and ideology) could be replaced by the semiotic. Now how does one come to explain the mother's eccentric gaze through the semiotic framework? For one, the mother in *Drought Victims* has the ability to look elsewhere, to separate her vision from the father's. It is then only fair to argue that *Drought Victims* presents the possible existence of female vision (vision which remains mysterious and therefore liberates itself from the patriarchal trap). Within Kristeva's theory, the mother's perceptual field indicates the possibility of an existence other than the one she is presently trapped in.

A simpler and more materialistic interpretation of the mother's vision in *Drought Victims* is that it signifies and therefore sheds light on her contradictory and impossible role in patriarchy.[23] In addition to the mother's perception being off center, the idea of hope seems to be encoded in her facial expression. Her very gaze seems to illuminate Shelley's wonderful phrase 'life is elsewhere.' When 'hope' and 'life is elsewhere' are brought together, two possible syntheses result: a) the hope that one day the subject in question may lead a better life, or b) the notion of woman as the bearer of hope i.e., of enduring in the anticipation of the future is another male construct. The thesis of this essay is, however, that cultural constructions ('ideological narratives') in representation are not always foolproof; consequently a weakness or blindspot in relation to perception exists in *Drought Victims* which could allow for a positive feminist analysis of the text.

The Construction Of Tragic Woman

The representation of tragedy in Lange's photography is of great interest because women are always the carriers. Kozol correctly observes in her essay on RA/FSA photography that "women most frequently appear unproblematically tragic and deserving of government assistance."[24] The mother in *Drought Victims* does not escape this systematic treatment of tragic representation. In the mother, three codes of expression can be read in the order of anxiety, worry, and hope. Kozol simply describes the mother as 'anxious looking' and with good reason—it is, after all, the dominant code of expression on her face. In looking at the mother, one almost feels the world might just collapse on her. It is this metaphorical code, which produces a specific feeling in a reader of the photograph, that determines her intense look into what has been described as the unlocatable, semiotic, or imaginary space. There is nothing positive, however, about disturbed thoughts (worry) being the determining factor in the mother's eccentric field of perception.

Moreover, to look elsewhere under the circumstances—to think that a better space or existence is to be located somewhere out of the present conditions—is absurd. Even the related thought that something outside of her present circumstances could come and help is unrealistic. The mother in *Drought Victims* is painted as a helpless creature who needs to look elsewhere in the midst of overwhelming conditions. The idea that there is hope in the distance is wishful thinking just as Kristeva's theory of the semiotic is. Positive change transpires only when a subject confronts and solves the negative qualities in his or her material circumstances. An important question nevertheless remains: Is the mother welcoming her tragedy? According to the French feminist thinkers discussed earlier the response would be negative because she looks elsewhere. For Kristeva and Irigaray, it at least signifies hope. Under the theoretical framework of this essay, it signifies nothing more than continued material oppression. One does not escape one's circumstances by dreaming of a possible outcome. The construction of tragic woman is, therefore, oppressive.

The most important question concerning *Drought Victims* is: What are the material causes that have led up to the family's tragedy? Are they (the family members) victims of a drought as Lange would have us believe, or are there political and economic forces behind their tragedy? Kozol argues the latter of the two possibilities for all the RA/FSA photography of the period. There is no reason to doubt this claim.

Consequently, it is clear that the photographic production of the RA/FSA always omitted the *true* material factors leading to the tragic and oppressive conditions of the people in the photographs. Tragedy, especially in *Drought Victims*, simply comes to serve as a universal signifier. The heavily determined code of the photograph is tragedy and it appears in its simplest, most *'natural'* form. This universalizing and naturalizing process of the tragic code was deemed of greater value by the RA/FSA than having the mother or father protesting their circumstances,[25] or having them point to the factors of their tragic oppression.

The mother, however, is not represented as protesting her circumstances; instead she is revealed within the constraints of the tragic pose. This latter depiction unquestionably satisfied the RA/FSA's general/official narrative. The RA/FSA not only did not take into account the material causes of tragedy and the possibility of 'protest' in the representation, but also allowed to slip away the realistic depiction of mother as worker of the fields. Not once does one get a glimpse of women's occupational activities in Lange's photography, and yet women were more than just mothers at the time. Kozol argues the point: 'Rural women did domestic chores and raised the children as well as tended the garden and livestock and worked in the fields.'[26]

Therefore mothers are not simply mothers in these photographs, but are, nevertheless represented as nothing other than mothers in order to satisfy the official narrative. In effect, Lange's *Drought Victims* produces the concept of mother through a lack of material specificity. This lack of specificity results in the creation of an abstract construction. Woman comes to signify nothing other than maternity and care.

Migrant Mother

The title of Lange's next photograph is worth considering. Why should it be titled *Migrant Mother* and not migrant mother with two children and one infant? It will be argued later in this section that the title simply over-determines what is already an ideologically charged photograph. In this section a description of *Migrant Mother* will precede a careful examination of the issues of ideological construction of woman, woman's oppression, and sexuality.

On each side of the mother, who takes up almost three quarters of the photograph, are her older children. Both children are leaning on her shoulders. The mother, once again, with a distressed look on her face seems to be staring out into an unknown space. She is holding, in her left hand, a dirty infant wrapped in rags. The mother's attire is not much better. Her sweater is torn at the elbows. The mother's right hand tentatively touches her chin. Only a bit of the tent and no other specific signs of their living conditions are displayed because of the close framing of the group. The mother is clearly the center of attention, especially since her other two children have their heads turned away. The close framing of half of the family in this case, because Kozol tells us there are another four children, gives the photograph an *oppressive air*. The space the mother is inhabiting is overwhelmingly oppressive, but she seems to be coping admirably under the circumstances. (This reading is up to debate. It is the kind of reading the RA/FSA would prefer but she can also be read as a living time bomb.) Unlike *Drought Victims*, there is no depth of space in *Migrant Mother*. Depth of field is, however, emphasized in the mother's vision. She seems to be staring into a far distance. Kozol says the mother is protecting her young. Is she? Or does she consider them oppressive and therefore has to look elsewhere.

The Construction Of Oppression

Even the most simple glance at *Migrant Mother* will bring to surface the notion of oppression. It is, in fact, an extraordinary document of the compositional construction of oppressive space. The parts that combine to form the whole are tightly squeezed into the frame. Who is oppressed? The mother is for two reasons: she is the only figure in the photograph we can directly identify with, and she is the one who has children from all angles forcing her into the constrained space of the center. *Migrant Mother*, at its most superficial level, seems to point to the mother's oppressive role in the patriarchal institution of the family. Is it not evident that she does not have room to breathe within the *frame* of the family? The cause of oppression, in the compositional structure of *Migrant Mother* (and most certainly in real life too) are the children hanging over the mother's shoulders. One look at *Migrant Mother* and one thinks of Dinnerstein and Chodorow thesis that the oppression of women originates in the female monopoly on mothering. She is, after all, represented alone with her three children. To think she may have more children is enough to make whomever knows it feel oppressed.

Migrant Mother is a crucial photograph to study because its very nature is, it would seem, contradictory. The contradiction, however, is a weak one. It has been argued that at one level, *Migrant Mother* serves as a document of woman's oppressive role in patriarchy. At a more profound level, it serves as part of the patriarchal conditioning process that will determine the very shape/structure of woman, in the present of the photograph (1930's), and in the future. The future of women's oppression is being designed in the present—in *Migrant Mother*. It is hard to say whether a real contradiction or whether true tension exists within the photograph because the latter, ideologically based reading is better reinforced. The patriarchal narrative of oppression is carried through because Lange has created a strong mother and impossible circumstances. That is, the mother gives the spectator the impression that she has the strength to bear such great oppression. Consequently the possibility of true tension in *Migrant Mother* is overwhelmed.

Migrant Mother is, then, another example of photographic construction which is determined by the hegemonic—the power bloc's wish to represent women's oppression as natural. After all, the woman in *Migrant Mother* is fixed into the role of mother in both image and title. The title *Migrant Mother* is of greater use when seen as language which helps to over-determine the already existing construction of a timeless and universal mother in the image. The title simply reinforces our reading of the image as that of the ever powerful and mythical mother. The creation of the mother in *Migrant Mother* overwhelms the rest of the parts in the composition. Motherhood then is universalized. And this particular oppressed mother is rendered timeless.

Does this not support the original claim: If the mother comes to represent all women, the consequences are simple, women are and will remain oppressed through the ages. *Migrant Mother* methodically forecasts future oppression. It does so through its timeless quality; that is, it could be displaced easily from the present context and placed into a future context.

Universality and timelessness are produced through the construction of codes of expression. Both *Migrant Mother* and *Drought Victims* have a universal timelessness about them. The result of such construction is the omission of material circumstances. Before speculating on what is omitted, it is worth examining the means by which Lange's photography achieves this timeless and universal quality. In *Drought Victims*, anxiety, worry, and hope can be read as the mother's codes of expression.

The father expresses simple despair. Codes, as is well known, are cultural constructions[27]; they ensure that most people in the social come up with similar interpretations of objects or events. Everyone is familiar with anxiety, worry, hope, and despair: these emotions or states will always be part of human consciousness. It is precisely this construction of 'foreverness' in *Drought Victims* which renders it eternal. It is interesting to consider that anxiety, worry, and hope are negative emotions and states; that is, they are inevitably associated with weakness. In contrast, despair can be interpreted as a positive state. That is, it is often seen to connote a 'realistic outlook' or 'strength of outlook.'[28] It is possible to argue then that the construction of gender is also fulfilled through codification: woman is weak, whereas man is realistic!

In *Migrant Mother* the mother's distressed yet strong, thoughtful look turn her into a monumental, and everlasting paradigm of the philosopher who endures pain. Finally, in the creation of universality and timelessness, something of great importance is forgotten: the social discrimination and the exploitive conditions the migrant mother and drought victims were forced to encounter.

The same argument that was made for *Drought Victims* in respect to field of vision also applies to *Migrant Mother*. The strength she embodies is further reinforced by her ability to look elsewhere—to dismiss through visionary perception her oppressive condition. It has already been observed how this kind of vision into the unknown can be interpreted through Kristeva's theory of semiotic space. Such a theoretical framework for feminist theory has also been criticized. There is nothing positive or realistic about turning one's eyes away from misery. To confront and to solve a problem, is positive. In short, then, a positive feminism, one which has actual material application, cannot be born out of the semiotic.

The Question Of Sexuality

Lack of sexuality is the best way to describe *Drought Victims*, *Migrant Mother* and *Wife of a Migrant Laborer*.[29] There is no hint of sexuality in expression, body, or contact in the subjects that are represented. The woman in *Drought Victims* does not express sensuality in any form, nor do the other women in *Migrant Mother* and *Wife*. Their bodies, it seems, have lost the capacity (due to the harsh conditions of oppressive motherhood and field work) to produce the vital energy that sexuality is normally affiliated with. Wendy Kozol accurately discusses the issue of sexuality in RA/FSA photography and also points to its definite connection with dominant ideology:

> There is little or no tenderness between husbands and wives; signs of intimacy exist only between parents and children. Rarely do images of mothers stress their sexuality, even when maternity is explicitly emphasized. Instead, the archetypal role of mother, *lacking*, sexuality and full of good moral values, was depicted in countless pictures of women surrounded by their children. "Madonnas of the Fields" were of critical importance in the RA/FSA narrative of poverty and need, for they constructed and reasserted dominant societal views on women and the family.[30]

But Kozol does not take her analysis of sexuality far enough: the production of bodies in RA/FSA photography systematically works to promote a repulsion response from the spectator. Why is this the case?

Ideology, The State And Sexuality

Nothing ever escapes ideology, not even the issue of sexuality. This is especially evident in the context of 1930's America. The U.S. experiences, at the time, a major economic crisis; the result of which is a country in disarray. The state slowly but surely had to secure means of controlling both the economy and its citizens. Somehow a balance had to be reached between high population numbers and very low employment. It is within this context that an explanation of the lack of sexuality in RA/FSA photograph is to be developed. Is not such representation of sexuality a symptom of the state's desire to discourage high birth rate in a period of economic crisis? It is well documented that the RA/FSA was a state-sponsored program. If the ideology of the state was to reduce birth rate, and indeed it was, Lange's photography can and must be seen as a calculated attempt, as an ideological document reinforcing reduced birth rate. The state thus controlled, to a great extent, the sexual conduct of the citizens of the time through the agency of Lange's photographs and the RA/FSA in general.

To be sure, the state must have made use of a whole arena of agencies, encompassing all areas of society, to produce and distribute the notion of 'asexuality.' In *The History of Sexuality: Volume 1*, Michel Foucault discusses the frequent use, in the twentieth century, of systematic campaigns that would try to establish an equivalence between the biological/sexual activity of its citizens and the economy:

> There also appeared those systematic campaigns which, going beyond the traditional means—moral and religious exhortations, fiscal measures—tried to transform the sexual conduct of couples into a concerted economic and political behaviour.[31]

And again, Foucault, on the state's method of invasion into the sexual realm:

> Between the state and the individual, sex became an issue, and public no less; a whole web of discourses, special knowledge, analyses and injunctions settled upon if.[32]

In essence, then, lack of sexuality in Lange's photography is state-determined. The ideological construct of 'Lack of sexuality' functions as one of the many ways in which the state tried to bring order to a chaotic imbalance between reproduction, the sexual body, and the economy.

Wife of a Migrant Laborer And Conclusion

Wife of a Migrant Laborer is not in the same category as *Drought Victims* or *Migrant Mother*. It is clearly not one of Lange's best photographs. The mythical nature of this photograph is all too obvious. In this simple example of myth-making, however, one notion is made clear: nothing is left to chance, nothing has been accidental in this specific example of Lange's work. A description of *Wife of a Migrant Laborer* will reveal its constructive quality.

The wife strikes a purely theatrical pose of tragedy and oppression against a deep, blue sky with only a hint of a cloud in it. She is older than the previous mothers we have described. This wife, unlike the other two, is no longer looking into any distance. Instead, her eyes remain shut. Her working outfit has been, like the migrant mother's, torn around the neck area. Another tear in the outfit is noticed under her left arm, which is holding her right arm. Her right hand mythically lays itself on her forehead. Behind her is a cornfield.

Wife of Migrant Laborer is chosen as a third example of Lange's photography because it is an obvious example of 'woman' and not 'women.' Throughout this essay the use of 'woman' has been used interchangeably with 'women' in the analyses of Lange's texts. In the theoretical discussions of feminism however, not once was the abstraction 'woman' used. This is of relevance because the thesis of this essay is that 'women'—the material, political, economic, and social oppression they experience—must at all times be emphasized at the expense of abstraction. To simply represent the signifier Woman, as is the case in *Wife of a Migrant Laborer,* is a grave injustice. One might instead wish to know what were the material conditions which led to her tragic pose. *Wife* is an example of the construction of tragic women, which translates to the construction of weak women in the social. The ideological narrative of the photograph is, after all, that wives of migrant laborers are in desperate need of help. In the construction process, as has been argued earlier, something is always omitted. In the case of *Wife*, it is the woman's occupational activities. A theatrical pose instead of the type of work she engages in is deemed of greater relevance to the construction of the official narrative. *Wife*, a lot like *Drought Victims* and *Migrant Mother*, also stimulates a repulsion-response from the spectator. The wife of the migrant laborer lacks all the sexuality and sensuality possible. It is important to keep in mind that not even 'female sexuality' escapes the male ideological construction process. If woman in Lange's photography is represented as 'lacking sexuality' it is because the state (a male institution) will insure its own views, needs, and interests, through such representations.

In conclusion, the thesis of the essay bears repetition, even though it applies mostly to *Drought Victims* and *Migrant Mother*: at one level Dorothea Lange's most recognized photographs systematically construct an oppressive narrative; at another level, however, they allow room for an interpretation of women's contradictory and impossible role in patriarchy.

Notes

1. "Woman" is used innocently at this stage of the essay. The term will however be problematised as the essay begins to concretely examine what some feminist theorists have had to say about what is ultimately an abstract construction. For a convincing argument against the use of "woman" in relation to actual female experience see Janet Todd's, *Feminist Literary History*, (New York: Routledge, 1988).

2. See Louis Althusser, "Ideology and Ideological State Apparatuses," in *Lenin and Philosophy and Other Essays*, (New York: Monthly Review Press, 1971), p. 162.

3. "Ideology and State Apparatuses," p. 164.

4. John Fiske, et al., *Key Concepts in Communication*, (New York: Mehtuen, 1983), p. 107.

5. *Key Concepts in Communication*, p. 107.

6. *Key Concepts in Communication*, p. 109.

7. *Key Concepts in Communication*, p. 103.

8. *Key Concepts in Communication*, p. 102.

9. Wendy Kozol, "Madonnas of the Fields: Photography, Gender and the 1930's Farm relief," in *Genders*, 2 (1988), p. 1.

10. *Key Concepts in Communication*, p. 103.

11. Janet Todd, *Feminist Literary History*, (New York: Routledge, 1988) p. 22.

12. See Elizabeth Wright's *Psychoanalytic Criticism*, (New York: Methuen, 1984), p. 110.

13. Rosemarie Tong, *Feminist Thought: A Comprehensive Introduction*, (Boulder: Westview Press, 1989), p. 96.

14. The idea here is once again taken from Rosemarie Tong's *Feminist Thought*, p. 96.

15. Kate Millet, *Sexual Politics*, (New York: Avon, 1971), p. 203.

16. *Feminist Thought*, p. 104.

17. The notion of blindspots, weaknesses, and gaps existing in all texts is examined in depth in Jacques Derrida's *Limited Inc.*, trans. Samuel Weber (Evanston, IL: Northwestern University Press, 1988). Another fine analyses of the above issue is to be found in Derrida's "Structure, Sign and Play in the Discourse of the Human Sciences," *Writing and Difference*, (Chicago: University of Chicago Press, 1978).

18. Todd, *Feminist Literary History*, p. 83-83.

19. *The Bible: New International Version*, (Grand Rapids, MI: Zondervan, 1973), p. 586.

20. Tong, *Feminist Thougbt*, p. 156.

21. Anika Lemaire, *Jacgues Lacan*, trans. David Macey (New York: Routledge, 1977), p. 127.

22. Todd, *Feminist Literary History*, p. 52.

23. For an interesting discussion of the subversive possibilities of female vision see Tania Modleski's *The Women Who Knew Too Much: Hitchcock and Feminist Theory* (New York: Routledge, 1988). For a specific discussion of how vision may be associated with women's contradictory role in a male world see p. 26 of the same book.

24. Kozol, "Madonnas of the Fields," p. 8.

25. "Madonnas of the Fields," p. 9.

26. "Madonnas of the Fields," p. 7.

27. For a strong analysis of the ways in which codes are cultural constructions see Roland Barthe's *Mythologies*, trans. Annette Lavers (London: Paladin, 1973).

28. It is possible to think of despair in a positive light. Alain Resnais, in one of his lesser known films, has one of his characters express the view that a strong subject is born out of having all of these four elements: cynicism, despair, strength, and humor.

29. *Wife of a Migrant Laborer* will simply be examined here as another explicit example of the construction process in Lange's photography.

30. Kozol, "Madonnas of the Fields," p. 13.

31. Michel Foucault, *The History of Sexuality: Volume 1,* trans. Robert Hurley (New York: Vintage, 1980), p. 26.

32. Foucault, *The History of Sexuality*, p. 26—27.

Bibliography

Althusser, Louis. *Ideology and Ideological State Apparatuses*, Lenin and Philosophy and other essays. Trans. Ben Brewster. New York: Monthly Review Press, 1971.

Barthes, Roland. *Mythologies*. trans. Annette Lavers. London: Paladin Books, 1973.

Dali, Mary. *Beyond God the Father: Toward a Philosophy of Women's Liberation*. Boston: Beacon Press, 1973.

De Lauretis, Teresa. *Alice Doesn't*. Bloomington: University of Indiana Press, 1988.

Douglas, Mary. *Purity and Danger: An Analysis of the Concepts of Pollution and Taboo*. New York: Praeger, 1966.

Foucault, Michel. *The History of Sexuality: Volume 1*. New York: Vintage Books, 1978.

Kozol. Wendy. "Madonnas of the Fields: Photo, Gender, and 1930's Farm Relief," *Genders*: 1988.

Luckmann, Thomas and Peter Berger. *The Social Construction of Reality*. New York: Penguin Books, 1966.

Millet, Kate. *Sexual Politics*. New York: Avon Books, 1970.

Modleski, Tania. *The Women Who Knew Too Much: Hitchcock and Feminist Theory*. New York: Routledge, 1988.

O'Sullivan, Tim, John Hartley, Danny Saunders and John Fiske. *Key Concepts in Communication*. New York: Methuen, 1983.

Todd, Janet. *Feminist Literary Theory*. New York: Routledge, 1988.

Tong, Rosemarie. *Feminist Thought: A Comprehensive Introduction*. Boulder: Westview Press, 1988.

Williams, Raymond. *Keywords*. London: Fontana Press, 1976.

Wright, Elizabeth. *Psychoanalytic Criticism, Theory in Practice*. New York: Methuen, 1976.

The Unconscious and Grotesque Aspect of Walt Whitman's *The Sleepers*

2

> A man tormented by physical and mental suffering obtains from dreams what reality denies him: health and happiness.
>
> —P. Radestock, *Schlaf Und Traum*

> The unfinished and open body (dying, bringing forth and being born) is not separated from the world by clearly defined boundaries: it is blended with the world, with animals, with objects. It is cosmic, it represents the entire material bodily world in all its elements. It is an incarnation of this world at the absolute lower stratum, as the swallowing up and generating principles, as the bodily grave and bosom, as a field which has been sown and in which new shoots are preparing to sprout.
>
> —M.M. Bakthin, *Rabelais and His World*

The Unconscious and Surplus Repression

The first stanza of Walt Whitman's *The Sleepers* situates the sleeper-persona, through whom we see things, within the context of dream:

> I wander all night in my vision,
> Stepping with light feet, swiftly and noiselessly
> Stepping and stopping,
> Bending with open eyes over the shut eyes of sleepers,
> Wandering and confused, lost to myself, ill-assorted,
> Contradictory,
> Pausing, gazing, bending, and stopping.[1]

The immediate signifiers of a dream landscape are "vision," "light feet," and "noiselessly stepping and stopping." A dream is always ever a vision, and "light feet" and noiseless stepping are symptomatic of the immaterial nature of psychical dream life. The fourth line of the stanza is, however, most convincing: the very anatomy and quality of dream is expressed in "lost to myself," "ill-assorted," and "contradictory." "Lost to myself" is poetic metaphor for Sigmund Freud's theory of how sleep and dream form the most narcissistic experience in human life.[2] Also descriptive of dreams is "ill-assorted" and "contradictory": both poetic usages in turn elucidate the fragmented structure of, and the illogicality of dream content. The "ill-assorted" (fragmented) form of a dream is best illustrated as follows:

A ➡ Z ➡ M ➡ Q

In dreams, then, "ill-assorted" material is brought together in illogical unity—in the unconscious' attempt to express a "contradictory" narrative. The "contradictory" structure of a dream, however, is only ever valid when examined in its relation to the material existence of waking life. In his journey into the night the sleeper-persona initially distinguishes the world of dream from the world of earthly existence, and then locates a space wherein this world lies:

> Now I pierce the darkness, new beings appear,
> The earth recedes from me into the night,
> I saw that it was beautiful, and I see that what
> Is not the earth is beautiful.
> Cache and cache again deep in the ground and sea,
> and where it is neither ground nor sea.[3]

The world of dream as the sleeper-persona indicates, requires a "piercing" into darkness where "new beings appear." Entrance into the dream involves a two-fold mechanism in which the sleeper-persona must disavow an absent daylight, and "pierce" through the darkness. The "piercing" effect is the conditional factor permitting the sleeper-persona penetration into a separate world. After disavowing and "piercing"—the sleeper, who is not yet the dreamer, sees the "earth recede from him into the darkness." During this instance of recession, the "distinctness" and "other worldliness" of the unconscious is materialized.

The unconscious is: the receding or withdrawal from the point which is earth and the entrance into the night, where it is "beautiful" and "new beings appear." (In Freudian theory and in Whitman's *The Sleepers* the system unconscious/night holds within it residue of consciousness/earth. This affect is most evident when the sleeper-persona states "the earth recedes...into the night.") The "newness" of this world of "otherness" propels in the sleeper-persona an excitation which conditions an attempt to describe its space of location. With vague incertitude the sleeper locates it, initially, somewhere hidden (cache and cache) "deep in the ground and sea." As soon as this indeterminate space is settled, a qualification follows: "it is neither ground nor sea." In the qualification the space of the unconscious is determined at yet another level, and its "location" is illustrated as follows:

> *Ground*
> *System UCS*...The unconscious occupies a space in between Ground and Sea
> *Sea*

Not to be reductive, however, this unconscious space is determined only in so far as it is free floating.

The Instinctual Life of the Dream

The role of the dream is to express that body of instinctual ideational content which normally undergoes repression. As Freud argues, in *Metapsychology,* dreams are best understood as expression-mechanisms of "the return of the repressed." Knowing this, an analysis of *The Sleepers* (the dream) reveals much about the sleeper-persona's unconscious instinctual life. The sleeper's dream reveals, for the most part, "unruly" and "unsociable" instinctual and ideational content. What is most *repressed* during the persona's waking life is *expressed* in his night life:

> The blind sleep, and the deaf and dumb sleep,
> The prisoner sleeps well in the prison, the runaway son sleeps,
> The murderer that is to be hung next day, how does he sleep?
> And the murder'd person, how does he sleep?[4]

In this compartment of the dream the "unruly" and "unsociable" is manifest in "prisoner," "runaway," "murderer," and "murder'd." In the eyes of waking life each of the above is a form or image of transgression, but within the context of dream each is awarded expression and appearance without an accompanying sense of guilt.

Two possible reasons for the "surfacing" of "unruly" and "unsociable" ideational content in the dream are "surplus repression" in the dreamer, and the latter's wish to transgress the limits or constraints of daily life. Although both interpretive strategies "seem" to be the same, the former provides a psychosomatic explanation, while the latter is purely concerned with psychical energy.

According to the psychosomatic explanation, the sleeper-persona's psyche and body—which suffer from too much repression—cannot withhold such unconscious material as "prisoner," "runaway," "murderer," and "murder'd person" from expression. In the former the sleeper's body and mind experience an explosion that is imagistically similar to an uncontrollable eruption. In the latter the persona is in the process of fulfilling a psychical wish. If waking life is too civil and conservative, the dream permits the sleeper-persona to transgress the rules of conduct, and to become the "runaway" and the "murderer."

Transgression and Wish Fulfilment: Homoeroticism

The primary formation of transgression, and revelation of wish fulfilment in the sleeper-persona's dream is the content of homoeroticism. The homoerotic, in the life of the dream, is primary not because of its quantitative amount, but due to its initiatory entrance. "Surplus repression" and homophobia elucidate best the conditioning base from which the sleeper's homoeroticism erupts.[5]

The early expression of homoerotic desire and experience transpire in the following verses: "Double yourself and receive me darkness, / Receive me and my lover too, he will not let me go without him." "He whom I call answers me and takes the place of my lover, / He rises silently with me from the bed," and "Darkness, you are gentler than my lover, his flesh was sweaty and panting, / I feel the hot moisture that he yet left me."[6]

In all three spurts of unconscious expression one constant remains: the sleeper-persona's "lover" is always a "he." The process characterized in the persona's homoerotic discourse involves a shift from an initial physical male sexual experience, to a symbolic male relationship with "darkness." (In fact, "darkness" is a complex substitution symbol for the material male lover). In this process of transference, it cannot be overlooked that the sleeper starts off with two male "lovers," "darkness" and "his lover," and ends with one: "darkness" alone. The "deed" has also been committed: the sleeper is located in "bed" with a male lover whose "flesh" is "sweaty and panting." The "deed" is finalized after the sleeper-persona exclaims: "I feel the hot moisture that he yet left me." The sleeper's desire, consequently in the dream, is to escape the imperfect eroticism of his physical male companion and to be taken away by the "gentler" male form of "darkness." The "process," "discourse," "deed," and "desire" of homoeroticism is afforded expression in the sleeper-persona's dream because, it would seem, sexuality of such kind is overly suppressed in waking life. If the sleeper is granted heterosexuality, *a priori*, then the expression of homoerotic love in his dream is potentially revelatory of a conscious life which represses greatly and fears such love. In consequence, what is repressed too much "returns" in uncontrollable abundance and excess in the dream. The sleeper's dream, then, is a transgression against the limits of waking life and a Wish Fulfilment of what that life denies him.

THE UNCONSCIOUS AND GROTESQUE 43

Violence and "The Dead"

The secondary quality of the ideational and instinctual life of the sleeper-persona's unconscious is violence. Quantitatively, images of brutality and violence compose the greatest part of the sleeper's dreamscape. In the "gigantic swimmer" segment of the dream the persona witnesses an episode of "individual violence":

> Steady and long he struggles,
> He is baffled, bang'd, bruis'd, he holds out while his strength holds out,
> The slapping eddies are spotted with his blood, they bear him away, they roll him, swing him, turn him,
> His beautiful body is borne in the circling eddies, it is continually bruis'd on rocks,
> Swiftly and out of sight is borne the brave corpse.[7]

In contrast to the sleeper's visions of homoerotic love this segment of the vision has an accompanying sense of anxiety: "I hate the swift-running eddies that would dash him head-foremost on the rocks."[8] Furthermore, the above is an explicit paradigm of the "death dream." The anxiety experienced by the sleeper is manifestly due to the visualization of the death of a "loved" one. Three factors lead to this deduction: first, the "gigantic swimmer" is male; second, this segment of the dream immediately follows the persona's homoerotic dream experiences; and third, before the above stanza the sleeper describes the figure of death as being "naked" in the sea and having "beautiful brown hair" and "courageous arms."

The sleeper-persona's description of the swimmer as male, and the location of the episode, betray a doubtless love affinity. According to Freudian dream theory, it is only natural to experience anxiety at the sight of the death of a "loved" one. The sleeper-persona, interestingly enough, also experiences an image of "collective violence"; it is the vision of a tempest destroying a ship and the crew members on board. This vision, like the vision of individual death and suffering, is fraught in brutal and aggressive imagery: "I look where the ship helplessly heads end on, I hear the burst as she strikes, I hear the howls of dismay, they grow fainter and fainter."

Throughout this vision of violence there is sadness, anxiety, and despair in the voice of the sleeper, but there is also the perverse—if not masochistic—need for it to be expressed. Violence and death—like homoeroticism—in themselves forms of transgression, surface uncontrollably in the persona's unconscious. It would seem, then, that the violent and aggressive instincts in the sleeper-persona do not undergo sublimated expression in conscious life and therefore erupt in the unconscious, where they are without harmful consequence to society. (At this point, it is necessary to discuss the Lacanian link of text and unconscious. For Lacan "the entire unconscious is structured like a language"[9]; thus the sleeper who "always already" experiences and exists in language is "always" in the realm of the unconscious. Such an equation, however, does imply that a text, like the unconscious, can not be a living threat to the social.) In relation to wish fulfilment, images of the death of a "loved" one translate to a repressed desire for the actual death of a loved one in the conscious life of the sleeper.

In the last part of section four, "the dead" appears in the sleeper-persona's dream discourse relating to the collective tragedy. At one level, it points to a possible desire to visualize and enact that which has not been experienced in waking life. "The dead" emerges out of the following context: "I search with the crowd, not one of the company is washed to us alive. / In the morning I help pick up the dead and lay them in rows in a barn."[10] Beyond being a powerful dream image, "the dead" is in every way associated with the unconscious; it is after all the "material unconscious" of civilisation. At another level, then, the sleeper's obsession with "the dead" is an obsession with mystery, knowledge, and certainty. In knowing that "the dead" possess what the living lack, the persona's dream takes on the form of a quest—of an Oedipal journey of clairvoyance.[11] A basic drive therefore conditions the surplus of death imagery: the drive is the wish to *know* what it is to be dead, or at least to know what the dead know. The "gaining" of such experience would result in the culmination of the sleeper-persona's obsessive desire to obtain totality.

Repress

Just as Washington "cannot repress" the tears from dropping, the sleeper-persona "cannot repress" the historical image of Washington's defeat:

> Now of the older war-days, the defeat at Brooklyn,
> Washington stands inside the lines, he stands on
> the intrench'd hills amid a crowd of officers,
> His face is cold and damp, he cannot repress the
> weeping drops,
> He lifts the glass perpetually to his eyes,
> the color is blanch'd from his cheeks,
> He sees the slaughter of the souther braves
> confided to him by their parents.
> The same at last and at last when peace is declared,
> He stands in the room of the old tavern, the

well-beloved soldiers all pass through,
The officers speechless and slow draw near
in their turns,
The chief encircles their necks with his arm
and kisses them on the cheek,
He kisses lightly the wet cheeks one right after
another, he shakes hands and bids good-by to
the army.[12]

If "what cannot be repressed" is descriptive of dreams, then the persona's vignette-like description of the revolutionary war is an unconscious utterance. There is—in the very fact of expression—a felt *need* to plunge into, once again, a historical fragment of the past. The vignette is therefore a historical experience—a residue of the sleeper's past which refuses to become "dormant" and continues instead to survive, in "detailed" form, in the unconscious. In its very expression the sleeper-persona's unconscious is fulfilling this utterance: I *need* to see and to experience again the military defeat of the revolutionary war. Consequently, in section five, a strong unconscious residue of the past attempts to push into consciousness the failure of the revolution.

Merge

The sleeper-persona pronounces—in section seven—one of the most revelatory statements concerning the unconscious. In a fit of joy, while mentioning the seasons, the astonishing pronouncement of "elements merge in the night" surfaces unexpectedly. According to the sleeper's discourse everything becomes one in the "night": "elements merge," equality is assumed, and "violent undifferentiation" exists. More emphatically, all "elements"—subjects and objects—suffer Baudrillardian "implosion": a complete regression to "equivalence" or as the sleeper-persona defines it "average," which in turn eventually leads to a single centre of chaos. In addition to "elements merge in the night" / unconscious, the sleeper superimposes another layer to his self-reflexive postmodernist theory of the unconscious: "And everything between *this* and *them* (my emphasis) in the dark, / I swear they are averaged now—one is no better than the other."[13]

If "this" is objects and "them" is subjects both the sleeper-persona and Baudrillard - whether it be through the use of the signifier "equivalence" or "averaged"—postulate the same notion in their "definitions" of the system unconscious. The persona-postmodernist reaches the penultimate point—the "finality"—of modern discourse after exclaiming "The diverse shall be no less diverse."[14] In the realm of the "night" / unconscious, "no longer" does the sleeper experience violent differentiation and distinction: "elements merge" to the point where they become "no less diverse."

More Or Less

In describing the "soul" as being more "or" less ("The soul is always beautiful, it appears more or it appears less, it / comes on or it lags behind") the sleeper continues to indulge in modern discourse. The "soul," in its unconscious state, is to be located, paradoxically, in a space of indeterminacy—without fixation in extent or character. It is this "or" it is that. In diagram form, the sleeper's theory of the "soul," is more "or" less something which is floating between two points.

What follows more "or" less ("it comes on or it lags behind") is vaguely indicative of what those two points might be: the present and the past "or" the future and the past. A "synthetic" (as in synthesis) view of the persona's description of the soul, however, gives precedence to this interpretation: the "soul" has "more" (the future) and "less" (the past), and something in between (the present). The soul therefore is like Carl Jung's theory of the unconscious—an unconscious which always, in its "prophetic" nature, envelopes the past, present, and future of the subject.

The Healing Powers of Sleep

> The mind has no wish to prolong the tensions of waking life; it seeks to relax them and to recover from them. It produces above all conditions contrary to the waking ones. It cures sorrow by joy, cares by hopes and pictures of happy distraction, hatred by love and friendliness, fear by courage and foresight; it allays doubts by conviction and firm faith, and vain expectation by fulfilment. Many of the spirit's wounds which are being constantly reopened during the day are healed by sleep, which covers them and shields them from fresh injury.
>
> —Sigmund Freud, *The Interpretation of Dreams*

Before his "awakening" ("I too pass from the night") the sleeper-persona uncannily reproduces, in his description of the effects of sleep, what Freud was to pronounce almost fifty years later.

> The sweating and fevers stop, the throat that
> was unsound is sound, the lungs of the consumptive
> are resumed, the poor distress'd head is free,
> The joints of the rheumatic move as smoothly as ever,

And smoother than ever,
Stiflings and passage open, the paralysed become
Supple,
The swell'd and convuls'd and congested awake
To themselves in condition.
They pass the invigoration of the night and the
chemistry of the night and awake.[15]

Disregarding some of the poetic excess, the persona's basic thesis is that sleep "invigorates" and has the effect of producing bio-chemical change which can lead to miraculous cures. Of course, the excess of the thesis—even "the paralysed become supple" —is generated by the sleeper-persona's two-fold wish that after the healing experience of sleep, the collective unconscious will awake and return to its duty of "hereditary perfection" and communal progress.[16] Most uncanny about the persona's theory of sleep is that it has been announced while still in a state of unconsciousness.

The Wait

Toward the conclusion of section seven, the words "wait" and "waits" appear repetitively. Clearly these words cannot, any longer, undergo repression, and therefore emerge, without restraint/economy in the sleeper-persona's unconscious discourse. This uncontrolled outpouring of wait/waits is symptomatic of a waiting period the collective body must experience. The waiting is a communal wait for those who "lag behind," or it is a case, as the sleeper describes it, of the "far advanced" who "wait" for the ill to recuperate:

The child of the glutton or venerealee waits long,
and the child of the drunkard waits long, and

> the drunkard himself waits long,
> The sleepers that lived and died wait,
> the fair advanced are to go on in their turns,
> and the far behind are to come on in their turns.[17]

The "waiting" period which sleep involves, it is hoped, will produce a total collective cure: "the diverse shall be no less diverse, but they shall flow and unite / they unite now."[18] The ill and the advanced, suddenly and miraculously, "unite" under the powerful command of the sleeper. The aim of the collective unconscious (unity) *was,* it seems, in a state of incompletion, non-fulfilment until the commandment "they unite now" *is* pronounced. Therefore, the role of the sleeper, both as one of the "advanced" and as a revolutionary who has been waiting, is to lift the weight of the past, and of "illness" off the shoulders of the collective. The wait/weight having now disappeared, can only be described as having been that of hereditary and communal imperfection.

The Grotesque Body

> I dream in my dreams all the dreams of the
> other dreamers, And I become the other dreamers.
> —Walt Whitman, *The Sleepers*

"I am" or "I become," in the sleeper-persona's dream discourse, are the linguistic signifiers of the grotesque concept of the body. In the above verse, the sleeper reveals himself to be that body which contains within it: all "otherness" ("I become the other dreamers"), and the totality of the collective unconscious ("I dream in my dreams all the dreams of the other dreamers"). Through introjection—a physical process whereby qualities that belong to an external object or subject are absorbed and unconsciously regarded as belonging to the self,[19] the persona tries to achieve what the grotesque body always ever aims to achieve: total absorption of the world. Complete/incomplete absorption of subjectivity transpires in the following stanza:

> I am the actor, the actress, the voter, the politician,
> The emigrant and the exile, the criminal that stood in the box,
> He who has been famous and he who shall be famous after to-day,
> The stammerer, the well-form'd person, the wasted or feeble person.[20]

Immediately after this intense grotesque implosion in which the persona is thirteen differing personalities he annunciates "I am she who adorn'd' herself and folded her hair expectantly"[21] as if to "rhetoricise" the idea of being all of subjectivity. "I am" subjectivity in its completion— is revelatory of the grotesque body which is always at least two, potentially more, and always incomplete (subjectivity only ever exists within the parameters of perpetual change and evolution), open, and unfinished.[22]

As the stanza indicates, in the grotesque body of the persona is born: woman and man ("actor"and "actress"), "criminal" and "well form'd person," the past and the present: ("He who has been famous and he who shall be famous after to-day.") (The unfinished and devouring nature of the grotesque body is evidently similar to the unconscious where it has been observed that all elements of the world "merge".)

To materialize and generalize the all enveloping and devouring nature of the persona's body "I am" or "I become" must be treated in relation to the world of objects. This paradox of completeness/incompleteness of the grotesque body is achieved when the sleeper declares: "A shroud I see and I am the shroud, I wrap a body and lie in the coffin."[23] In this instance, the persona—if he can still be called that—transcends subjectivity and becomes, in the purest form, an object. Thus, the persona's body fulfills all the qualities of the grotesque: it grows as it blends into itself all elements—subjects and objects—that the world has to offer. Interestingly enough, the potential appearance of the grotesque body is appropriately given shape by the grotesque utterance "my sinews are flaccid" which surfaces out of the sleeper-persona's mouthhole.

The sleeper's grotesque body is the physical counterpart (double) of *his* unconscious.

Notes

1. Walt Whitman, *Leaves of Grass and Selected Prose* (New York: McGraw Hill, 1981), p. 330—31.

2. Sigmund Freud, *The Interpretation of Dreams*, trans. James Strachey (New York: Pelican Books, 1976) p. 623.

3. Whitman, *Leaves of Grass,* p. 331, 32.

4. *Leaves of Grass*, p. 331.

5. It is taken for granted that Whitman's sleeper-persona is male. Much of *Leaves of Grass* and specifically "The Sleepers" gives the impression that the voice of the poem is simply an extension of Whitman.

6. *Leaves of Grass*, p. 332.

7. *Leaves of Grass*, p. 334.

8. *Leaves of Grass*, p. 334.

9. Jacques Lacan, *Ecrits*, trans. Alan Sheridan (London: Tavistock Publishers, 1977), p. 27.

10. *Leaves of Grass,* p. 334.

11. Harold Aspiz illuminates the ways in which Whitman engages in journeys of clairvoyance in his excellent work, *Walt Whitman and the Body Beautiful*, (Chicago: University of Illinois Press, 1980), p. 172.

12. *Leaves of Grass*, p. 334.

13. *Leaves of Grass*, p. 335.

14. *Leaves of Grass*, p. 337.

15. *Leaves of Grass,* p. 337.

16. The revolutionary and communal issue in Whitman is examined in Betsy Erkila's "The Federal Mother: Whitman as Revolutionary Son," *Prospects*, 10 (1985).

17. *Leaves of Grass,* p. 337.

18. *Leaves of Grass*, p. 337.

19. For a more complete definition of introjection see Elizabeth Wright's *Psychoanalytic Criticism: Theory in Practice* (New York: Metheun, 1984) p.80.

20. *Leaves of Grass*, p. 332.

21. *Leaves of Grass,* p. 332.

22. Mikhail Bakhtin, *Rabelais and His World,* trans. Helène Islwolsky (Bloomington: Indiana University Press, 1984), p. 26.

23. Op. cit., p. 333.

Bibliography

Aspiz, Harold. *Walt Whitman and the Body Beautiful.* Chicago: University of Illinois Press, 1980.

Bakhtin, Mikhail. *Rabelais and His World.* trans. Helène Islowlsky. Bloomington: Indiana University Press, 1984.

Baudrillard, Jean. *Simulations.* trans. Paul Foss, Paul Patton, and Philip Beitchman. New York: Semiotexte, 1983.

Bloom, Harold. *A Map of Misreading.* New York: Oxford Press, 1975.

Erkila, Betsy. "The Federal Mother: Whitman as Revolutionary Son." *Prospects 10*, 1985.

Freud, Sigmund. *The Interpretation of Dreams.* trans. James Strachey. New York: Pelican Books, 1976.

On Sexuality. trans. James Strachey. New York: Pelican Books, 1977.

Civilization, Society and Religion. trans. James Strachey. New York: Pelican Books, 1977.

Girard, Rend. *Violence and the Sacred.* trans. Patrick Gregory. Baltimore: Johns Hopkins Press, 1977.

Lacan, Jacques. *Ecrits,* trans. Alan Sheridan. London: Tavistock Publishers, 1977.

Miller, Edwin H. *Walt Whitman's Poetry: A Psychological Journey.* Boston: Houghton Mifflin Company, 1968.

Moon, Michael. *Disseminating Whitman: Revision and Corporeality in Leaves of Grass.* Cambridge, Mass.: Harvard University Press, 1991.

Whitman, Walt. *Leaves of Grass and Selected Prose.* New York: McGraw Hill, 1981.

Wright, Elizabeth. *Psychoanalytic Criticism: Theory in Practice.* New York: Methuen, 1984.

Variations on the Locomotive
and Landscape In George Inness'
Delaware Water Gap
and *Lackawanna Valley*

3

Write the vision, and make it plain.

—Habakkuk 2:2, King James Version of the Bible

For, as it is dislocation and detachment from the life of God that makes things ugly, the poet, who reattaches things to nature and the whole—reattaching even artificial things, and violations of nature, the nature, 'by a deeper insight'—disposes very easily of the most disagreeable facts. Readers of poetry see the factory village and the railway, and fancy that the poetry of the landscape is broken up by these; for these works of art are not yet consecrated in their reading; but the poet sees them fall within the great order not less than the bee hive or the spiders' geometrical web. Nature adopts them very fast into her vital circles, and the gliding train of cars she loves like her own.

—Ralph Waldo Emerson, The Poet

Art of whatever kind bears witness to intact objects even when the subject-matter is disintegration, whatever the form of transcript the original conservation as restoration is of the mother's body.

—Adrian Stokes, *Art and the Mind*

This essay, like all other essays I have written, may easily be criticized as 'lacking rigor.' A positivist will see no value in the excursions, experiments, and digressions that are to follow. And the writer of this essay, in turn, sees the positivists' task of recognizing *only* positive facts and observable phenomena oppressive, and potentially delusive.[1] This writer is not blessed with a strict, logical, scientific mind, but is, instead, inclined to fall deeply into the depths of creative gameplaying. At no point will he pretend that his work has any connection to the "real," nor will an attempt be made to follow the form and aim of conventional academic essay writing. The concrete center, which will hold this essay together, is nothing more than the objects of study: George Inness' *Delaware Water Gap* and *Lackawanna Valley*. Essentially, then, that which will be eternally absent in this essay is a strong system or structure enveloping the concrete centres. This is not to say, however, that the writer of this essay will shy away from constructing general, and smaller "frames of reference" from which to work.

Introduction

Of all sciences, the science of method attracts me most. I am strongly committed to presenting the ideas that are to follow in an orderly arrangement. I will begin this essay by constructing two frames of reference; the appellation of each to be pastoralism and transcendentalism. I will return to these general frames throughout the essay. Smaller frames will also appear: they will function as "bodies of ideology" to be applied to, and bounced off, the "concrete centres." These "bodies of ideology" will, simultaneously, operate as analytical tools and as absurdities; that is, when bounced off the "concrete centres," they will, in some instances, suddenly and surprisingly, uncannily reveal themselves to be "bodies of absurdities." For *Delaware Water Gap*, the smaller frame will contain Adrian Stokes' psychoanalytic interpretation of art and aesthetics. *The Lackawanna Valley* will be approached through Umberto Eco's and Roland Barthes' semiotic understanding of the nature and function of ambiguity in aesthetic practice. As the reader already begins to sense, the form of this essay will be essentially simple: frames of definition (pastoralism and transcendentalism) and bodies of ideology will appear before each detailed description of the texts of study. After describing, and to some extent "narrativizing" *Delaware Water Gap* and *Lackawanna Valley*, I will then proceed to examine each in relation to the established theoretical models on hand.

The analytic section of this essay will also rely heavily on a solid, more specific base, provided by: Leo Marx's *The Railroad-in-the-Landscape: An Iconoloaical Reading of a Theme in American Art*, Nicolai Cikovsky's *The Lackawanna Valley: Type of the Modern*, and Barbara Novak's section on "Trains" in *Nature and Culture*.

The aims of the essay have been implicitly brought to the fore: three areas of concern will compose and condition it: one, a concrete analysis, with a primary focus on content, of George Inness' *Delaware Water Gap* and *The Lackawanna Valley* in relation to Leo Marx's, Nicolai Cikovsky's and Barbara Novak's literature on the subject; two, a desire on the part of the writer to apply a general, all-enveloping theory of art to the texts; and three, to criticize and deconstruct systematically any theoretical or interpretive constructions which reveal hopeless weaknesses and blindspots when applied to the texts. Finally, the writer will admit a preference for an eclectic approach, which borrows significantly from psychoanalytic and semiotic theory and criticism.

Frame 1: The Pastoral Mode

I will turn to J.A. Cuddon's *A Dictionary of Literary Terms* for a comprehensive definition of the pastoral mode. From its inception, the pastoral, in literature and in art, shared similar features and concerns. It is, therefore, not of crucial importance to acknowledge separate definitions, separate categories of the genre, because of minute differences located in each of the two distinct modes of representation. J.A. Cuddon's understanding of the pastoral mode begins with a return to its origin.

Born out of the Latin, the signification of pastoral is "pertaining to shepherds." This knowledge leads Cuddon to state that the pastoral is: "a minor but important mode which, by convention, is concerned with the lives of shepherds."[2] More importantly, it tends toward an idealization of shepherd life, and, by so doing, "creates an image of a peaceful and uncorrupted existence."[3] Like all genres, the pastoral was fraught with great change and growth throughout its history. It is during the Christian phase that the notions of tranquility and harmonious love gain ground in the pastoral aesthetic. According to Cuddon, the coming of Christ and the consequent understanding that he was the shepherd and human beings were his flock, only made certain what was almost already certain in the minds of artists preoccupied with the pastoral mode: that the shepherd's life was a paradigm of harmony, tranquility, and peace.[4] In its fullest and most fundamental meaning, however, the pastoral aesthetic displays:

> ...a nostalgia for the past, for some hypothetical state of love and peace which has somehow been lost. The dominant idea and theme of the mode is the search for the simple life away from the court and town, away from corruption, war, strife, the

love of gain, away from 'getting and spending.' In a way, it reveals a yearning for a lost innocence, for a pre-fall paradisal life in which man existed in harmony with nature.[5]

It is fair to deduce, then, from the above, that the pastoral genre is a form of primitivism and its generating factor is a strong longing for things past. This simplicity and nostalgia, in turn, lead to the following formulation: as a genre, the pastoral is governed and generated by a desire to escape everything which has to do with the symbolic order of the social.

The pastoral poem and artwork was not always about "pastors," that is, shepherds, and their lives. In William Wordsworth's poetry, for instance, a variety of other rural themes and scenes are treated. More importantly, however, by the time Wordsworth is writing, the pastoral ideology and mode has experienced outstanding revolutionary change. In 1714, John Gay inadvertently paved the way, in his *Shepherd's Week*, toward a seriously realistic treatment of rural subject matter. But the true father—causing the permanent spread of realism in the pastoral aesthetic—was George Crabbe. Most of Crabbe's verse annals were outstanding for their realistic treatment of a variety of rural scenes, and his 'As truth will paint it and as bards will not,'[6] quickly became a rallying cry for the movement. For Crabbe, then, it was not only possible, but imperative, that the pastoral artist learn how to treat his subject matter without the idealism and formalism associated with the genre in its earlier phase.

In the case of the pastoral, we have seen how, by the eighteenth century, it adopts the realistic mode. This adoption, consequently, is causally responsible for growth and variety in the genre's subject matter. In light of this awareness, it will be of great interest to see how Inness' paintings, steeped in a pastoral realism, push the genre, in progressive spirit, to yet another level.

Many pastoral paintings fall under the spell of the sublime. George Inness' *Delaware Water Gap* is a strong example of the "pastoral sublime." The "pastoral sublime," as I will show shortly, is not necessarily a pasting together of two separate concepts. In fact, one look at Harold Bloom's interpretation of the sublime reveals an uncanny semblance between the sublime and the pastoral.

In *Poetry and Repression* and *A Map of Misreading*, Bloom sets out to explain the psychical strategies and experience "necessary" for the creation of sublime poetry. According to Bloom, the theme of a "natural innocence" regained is one that haunted the imaginations of all those Romantic and post-Romantic poets, from William Blake to Wallace Stevens. The poets he inspects suffer a condition of "belatedness"; that is, their arrival, like ours, occurs after the fall. It is, indeed, the "realizing point" in the realization of such a condition, and the consequent battle against it that brings about the genesis of sublime art. In Christopher Norris' words, the sublime, for Bloom, is "a quest for lost origins which the strong poet always engages in, though aware that his belated condition puts it beyond reach of any but the subtlest tropes and displacement(s)."[7]

The similarity between pastoral art and artist and sublime art and artist according to Bloom's conception of the latter is obvious: both are conditioned and propelled by desire: the desire for a return to the paradisal garden.

Frame 2: Transcendentalism

> Standing on the bare ground—my head bathed by the blithe air, and uplifted into infinite space—all mean egotism vanishes. I become a transparent

eyeball; I am nothing; I see all; the currents of the Universal Being circulate through me; I am part and parcel of God.

—Ralph Waldo Emerson, *Nature*

Barbara Novak provides an excellent introduction into the ideology of Transcendentalism in her book on American nineteenth century paintings. Novak's main thesis is that through Transcendentalism, one could indulge in a philosophical as well as physical union of idea and thing.[8] To the transcendental eye and mind, therefore, "object and idea were one." A further constituent element of the ideology, argues Novak, was an extreme emphasis on the "mystical fusion of God and nature."

By the mid-nineteenth century, under the influence of transcendental thought, all matter—whether animate or inanimate—was thought to be an extension of God, and therefore, it naturally came to signify His presence. (The radical nature of transcendental thought is worth exploring: as a "body of ideology" it presents us with a "multiplicity of mirroring." Both philosophy and the physical, God, man, and nature, essentially function as unmediated reflections of each another.) Also part of the ideology was Emerson's emphasis on "spirit in matter."[9] Many sources, including Inness' work, fostered a deep sense of an infinite life and spirituality in all matter. For the transcendentalists, then, matter, because it was infused with life and spirit, "could transform" and transcend its mere materialism, to become something psychical, and this, in the most human sense of the word. (It is possible to deduce, consequently, that Transcendentalism was an intellectual discourse and way of life in which the structure of idea-human-spirit assumed sublime status.) Thus, the logical consequence of the role of Emersonian Transcendentalism was to expose the "Eleusinian mysteries" which existed within the "stark common sense" of matter. Moreover, one of the most crucial concepts in Emersonian ideology was the "moment of juncture": that moment when the real and the ideal collide, and in effect become "part and parcel" of "the whole."

An analysis of Emerson's "transparent eyeball" passage will clarify and bring together the concerns of transcendental thought. Emerson begins his revelation with the physical ("standing on the bare ground"). Before he reaches the philosophic ("I become a transparent eyeball") he addresses infinity. Immediately after acquiring the philosophic, a union occurs between it and the physical. The union is so overwhelming that everything to follow is nothing more than the language of union—of transcendence. But what is the condition which permits Emerson to attain epiphanic union, and what is the consequence?

Union is achieved through the subtlest of tropes: that is, through the dislocation of head from body. "Bathed in blithe air" the head uplifts itself, only to become "a transparent eyeball" in the wandering realm of infinity. (In its very essence, the transparent eyeball is a displaced signifier of the transcendental "head.") The consequence of union is simple: the self as a *distinct* body vanishes. In fact, the precondition for transcendental vision and experience is rooted in a "vanishing of self." The self vanishes ("I am nothing"), so that whatever remains can become everything—that is, "part and parcel" of God, nature, and the "Universal Being."

Transcendental experience, in a word fusion, therefore, depends upon the greatest of paradoxes: the self must vanish for it to become part of "the whole." In short, Emerson's "transparent eyeball" is a sublime paradigm of the central concerns of Transcendentalism: the union of the *Its*, emphasis on infinity, the fusion between God, nature, and man, and the moment of juncture.

Delaware Water Gap (1857)

The Sky: The sky, in *Delaware Water Gap* fills up about half of the composition. The west is clean and clear with only a few scattered, almost invisible, clouds. The beautiful blue, between the patches of greyish-white matter is soothing to look at. It is difficult to tell, however, if the good weather of the west (left background) will slowly invade the east (right background). That which is certain is that the east is not blessed with a clear sky. For the most part (about three-quarters of the canvas), thick cloudy formations dominate. The far right corner is steeped in a threatening grey. The question to ask is: does the east bring with it "bad weather?"

The Landscape: It is beautiful to look at—a lot like a voluptuous woman's body. In the distance, from the right, all the way past the middle and into the left half of the canvas, a long, green, absurdly straight (equivalent in height) hill dominates. It is, along with a similar hill in the left middleground, the point of contact between itself (the landscape) and the sky. Four homesteads and a possible chapel are sprinkled across the widespread land. A gap exists between the two hills. In between this gap, a sparkle of royal blue is noticed in the distance.

In the left and right parts of the background, before the hills, the land seems to have been cleared, cultivated, for human purpose. In fact, the landscape as a whole is one of civilization. Patches of impressionistic, loosely painted trees appear in the background, sometimes in the midst of fields. To the right foreground, the natural environment has been virtually left untouched, except for two relatively inconspicuous baldspots. The adjacent ground is meadowy: the land is low—at the same level as the river—and flat. It seems to be simple grassland which is used for human purpose.

Most of the land described so far is represented in a greenish-yellowish color. In the left foreground, however, a brownish-yellow is most evident. Here, we experience the oak tree, the forest, the wheatfield, the grass, the pine tree, and the rocks overlooking the river, in as great detail as one will ever experience in Inness' art. The oak tree is of especial interest; its presence, in the middle of the wheatfield, in the left foreground, is conspicuous.

The River: It is, undoubtedly, the first thing one looks at. The elongated 'S' curve on the left side, the body of water, and the linearity of the right bank make the river look like a pregnant woman's body. In the right middleground behind the bridge, one notices a greenish layer of froth along the river's edge. The water is perfectly still. So still, that the trees in the left middleground and the bridge the train crosses over find their perfect reflection in the water. The river evokes a sense of tranquility, or as Leo Marx would have it "meandering ease."[10] The water simply flows quietly through a land without evident conflict, disorder, or anxiety. If we follow the river's curve, it leads us straight into the distance, precisely where the gap is found between the hills. The west side of the river is bathed in a clear blue color, whereas the east side is composed of different and less translucent shades of green. Almost one-quarter of the painting is filled by the stillness of the water.

The Train: A quick glance at *Delaware Water Gap* and one could never tell a train is travelling east to west, across the landscape. The "machine" blends as inconspicuously as possible into its natural surroundings. It is only a minuscule little engine "placed" in the middleground of the painting.

The little engine and its train of six cars has, only a moment ago, crossed the bridge overlooking the river. An area of thick woods is ahead. The train is about to enter, pass through this long stretch. Even from our vantage point, which is from a significant distance, we can still notice the train's energetic puffs of gentle, clean, white smoke. This train and its cars is depicted in such a manner as to make it unobtrusive, unthreatening, and certainly—because of the distance—inaudible.[11]

Inness has made it very clear: the new technology is perfectly in harmony with the basic flow and rhythm of the natural world. Still, the train does not transmit any signs of weakness amidst the "blending." Even in its minuscule form, it is irreducibly strong and committed.

Human Activity: Human design and activity has just about made its mark everywhere in *Delaware Water Gap*. The landscape is, after all, one of cultivated fields, with only a few "wild" spots. Even the river is a means toward a human productive end. In the middle of the river one notices a barge (a long flatbottomed boat for carrying freight on canal or river[12]) with five persons on it. A lot like a flying saucer, it seems to be suspended in mid-air.

But the most fascinating detail of human production and progress is revealed in the form of the reapers, in the left foreground. The two men are seen, amidst the wheatfield, cutting the crop, in a silence, humility, and light which transmits a quasi-religious aura. Their progress is from right to left, a lot like the train's. In fact, the direction of each, being so similar, forces one to conclude that an uncanny affinity exists between them.

More important than the train/reapers connection, however, is the way all human activity blends so perfectly and harmoniously in the tranquil landscape. This "blending" of man, technology, nature and God is, in its essence, the artistic representation of transcendental fusion. The reapers in the foreground and the workers on the barge finally remind us of that great pastoral desire "for a pre-fall paradisal life in which man existed in harmony with nature."

In studying Inness' work, one needs to examine his style, especially since it differs so radically from all other American painters of his time. Inness was and still is considered the greatest American stylist of the nineteenth century in the landscape mode of painting. Even in *Delaware Water Gap*, an early Inness painting, it is easy to see a distinctive stylistic approach to his medium. *Delaware Water Gap* is indeed one of Inness' most detailed representations. It is painted, according to Nicolai Cikovsky, Jr., "with a delicacy of color and a meticulous, controlled handling and attention to detail."[13]

Delaware Water Gap is, undoubtedly concerned with "precision and polished smoothness," but this is only true when examined within the context of Inness' art. Once outside his art, once compared to paintings of the same period and similar subject by contemporaries such as Thomas Cole and Asher B. Durand, it is easy to see that detail did not concern Inness as much as "a large vision and a poetic insight to the interpretation of the casual."[14]

Unlike the light brushwork and hyper-descriptive nature of Cole's and Durand's art, Inness brings a loose brush stroke and a slightly more subjective vision to a painting which, nevertheless, portrays, with great effort, accurately the topographical details of the *Delaware Water Gap*.

In writing about the Delaware Water Gap, Marx descnbes nicely the crucial difference between Inness' style and The Hudson River Schools:

Although *Delaware Water Gap* portrays a detailed view that includes figures, houses, a train, and a barge, Inness did not paint it with the tight, invisible brushwork typical of the Hudson River School.[15]

Subjective transcription was, then, of uppermost concern for Inness. In *Delaware Water Gap* Inness' considerable emphasis on style—on "manner and kind of expression"—illustrates itself in a lighter and freer use of the brush. The excessive brightness and luminosity of the aforementioned painting is another symptom which separates Inness from his fellow artists.

In short, then, the very style and look of *Delaware Water Gap* almost pre-figure what is later to be labelled Impressionist art, and, on the other hand it is only very distant in its connection to the Hudson River School style. As Cikovsky, Jr. points out, two words describe perfectly Inness' style: broad and allusive.

Paintings like the *Delaware Water Gap* are representations of the American pastoral landscape style. What is most important about the pastoral landscape style is that, in its very essence, it comes to include notions of the sublime and Transcendentalism. An examination of the genre, and its consequent application to *Delaware Water Gap* should, therefore, reveal a neat harmony between pastoral landscape, the sublime, and transcendental thought. Unfortunately, such an ingenious connection, of seemingly separate concepts, is not a chance construction by the writer of this essay. The landscape mode in painting has, from its inception, been affiliated with the pastoral genre in literature. Hence the inevitable outgrowth: "pastoral landscape." (Although it must be made clear that the "pastoral landscape" is only a compartment of the larger whole of the landscape mode.) Furthermore, the beautiful and the sublime has, forever, had the uncanny capacity to inscribe its presence in most modes of art, but especially in the landscape. And by the time Emerson and his followers appear on the scene, Transcendentalism only ever comes to signify itself through experience in "the landscape."

To be sure the above common links are too simple, not concrete enough, and infantile in scope. It is imperative that I reveal a stronger and more concrete link. To do so, Leo Marx's understanding of the aim of landscape painting must be examined. Marx argues, in *The Railroad-in-the-Landscape*, that the tacit aim of the landscape painting "had been to disclose the inherent beauty, order, and harmony of the natural environment."[16]

Marx later connects the motive behind landscape painting with that of the pastoral: "It (landscape painting) was closely akin to the pastoral mode in literature, whose central motive was a quasi-religious ideal of harmony, or reconciliation between man and nature."[17] Kenneth Clark's observation adds another important dimension to the genre: "the inception of landscape painting as a distinct form was closely tied to the image of an enchanted, paradisiacal garden."[18] For Clark, the landscape painting is "a flowery meadow" cut off from "the world of fierce accidents, where love...could find fulfilment."[19] Clark also notes that "paradise" is the Persian word for "a walled enclosure."

Marx and Clark's observations on the landscape genre in painting have made so much clear: as a form of art, the landscape painting is undeniably linked to the pastoral, to notions of the sublime, and to transcendental philosophy. If, then, we take the landscape (*Delaware Water Gap*) as our point of departure, or as our "concrete centre," we must then come to accept that seemingly foreign bodies like the sublime, pastoralism, and Transcendentalism inevitably link up, inside the centre, and become the constituent parts that give "whole" meaning to it. This model of understanding the pastoral landscape can only find validity when examined in relation to the concrete object of analysis, that is, *Delaware Water Gap*.

As I have made clear in the earlier blocks of this essay, "harmony or reconciliation" between "man and nature" is a desire and a belief held dearly by both pastoralists and transcendentalists. In *Delaware Water Gap*, perfect harmony is achieved between man, nature, and, in addition, technology.[20] That is, the train, the reapers, the barge and its' members, the scattered homesteads, the river, the land, and the sky blend into one another so neatly that they come to create a single whole.

The next link to be made is between the pastoral landscape, as paradisiacal garden, and the sublime. We have seen how, in Bloom's view, the generation of sublimity is achieved through an unconscious "working out" of the artist's strong desire for a return to the sublime moment of Edenic bliss. The link between Bloom's sublime, the pastoral, and the landscape mode is, therefore, clear, but a question remains unanswered: where and how does the sublime figure in the *Delaware Water Gap*?

Even Bloom's discourse on the sublime would seem to translate, in art, into the representation of other-worldly perfection. *Delaware Water Gap* achieves sublimity through two means: one, it gives the impression that it is a world cut off from "fierce accidents"; and two, through excessive brightness and luminosity. *Delaware Water Gap* very simply transcends the beautiful and ordinary to enter into a sphere of paradisal perfection—to become a representation of the "sublime topos" (Elysian Fields), as Marx would have it.

Although it is wise to think of the *Delaware Water Gap* as a pastoral landscape painting, it is even more necessary to stimulate a discourse which is less general. The very description of *Delaware Water Gap* betrays a simplistic, somewhat reductive reading of the painting as merely a representation of the pastoral landscape mode.

Is it not clear that more than just land appears in *Delaware Water Gap*? Another glimpse at the painting and one notices a train, the bridge that allows the train to cross over the river, a barge, humans, and scattered houses across the land. The label, "American pastoral landscape style" is, therefore, not complete; it does not, in any way, capture the "wholeness" of the subject. It is necessary, then, to work towards a more concrete definition of the mode *Delaware Water Gap* confronts us with. Cikovsky, Jr. and Marx have done admirable work in realizing the necessity for a more concrete method of probing the subject.

In his close scrutiny of the painting, Cikovsky, Jr. decides, intelligently enough, to place it within a tradition of painting which he calls "the civilized landscape." Cikovsky's descriptive phrase already brings us much closer to the truth of *Delaware Water Gap*. The painting is, after all, a glaring example of how nature is used and organized by human reason for human design. Of even greater importance, however, is that the term—"landscape of civilization"—somehow easily and harmoniously links that which is a construction of civilization, for instance, the train, with its very opposite nature.

In order to provide his coinage the necessary weight and strength to pass an acid test, Cikovsky, Jr. turns to Inness for help. According to Cikovsky, Jr., Inness, not only in *Delaware Water Gap* but in almost all his paintings, was essentially concerned with the representation of "civilized landscape." Cikovsky quotes Inness on the type of "civilized landscape" *Delaware Water Gap* represented in order to support his thesis:

I love it more and think it more worthy of reproduction than that which is savage and untamed. It is more significant. Every act of man...marks itself wherever it has been. [21]

Indeed, *Delaware Water Gap* does describe a scene where populated and depicted acts and emblems of civilization leave their mark throughout. We can infer, therefore, that "civilized landscape" is, in its most essential form, nature shaped by creative intelligence.

Three glaring signposts of "creative intelligence" exist in *Delaware Water Gap*: the train, the bridge, and the cultivated fields. All three signposts of technology work towards a creative and technological interpretation of the natural environment. (Although seemingly pedantic, all of the above is to indicate the writer's desire to begin a process of deconstructing the general, to break it into smaller units, so that we may acquire a more detailed and accurate language with which to analyze *Delaware Water Gap*.) Inness' *Delaware Water Gap* is, consequently, a strong example of the "civilized landscape" mode—a mode which reveals "human creativity" in the landscape, and the appearance of technology.

Similar to Cikovsky, Jr.'s civilized landscape is Marx's "landscape of reconciliation," another coinage used to describe the type of representation depicted in *Delaware Water Gap*. Unlike any other phrase, landscape of reconciliation seems to capture and describe accurately the subject in Inness' painting. For Marx, a landscape of reconciliation describes, in art, the achievement of a sense of harmony—a sort of union—between technology (trains in particular) and nature.

Such paintings—and *Delaware Water Gap* is a prime example of the genre—argues Marx, manifest quite clearly the artist's desire to preserve "the transcendental whole."²² Everything in the landscape of reconciliation assumes an overwhelming equivalence: everything—from the river, to the train, to the land—falls into a perfect, compliant transcendental union.

Of course, Marx's descriptive phrase for *Delaware Water Gap* and other paintings of the genre, reminds us of Emerson's passionate prescription for the artist who is confronted with new social phenomena. Emerson, as I quoted at the very start, sees the poet as one who is capable of, and indeed must be willing to, depict the train and the "factory village" within the "great order" (nature).

Therefore, the role of the artist, in Emerson's estimation, is to depict typical scenes of the era, but to depict them from a transcendental viewpoint: that is, from an ideal, affirmative viewpoint.23 So that if the train, for example, is a typical scene of the new era, and indeed it was by 1857, an Emersonian painting should labor towards appropriating it within the existing structure of the transcendental whole.

Transcendentalism is an ideological body which thrives on a perpetual state of engulfment, engulfing external, seemingly foreign "anti-bodies" and making them "part and parcel" of its wholeness. Both *Delaware Water Gap* and Arthur B. Durand's *Progress,* epitomize the Emersonian ideal of a "landscape of reconciliation."²⁴ In *Delaware Water Gap*, a strong reconciliation, harmony, and compatibility exist between the natural and technical. It is interesting to note, however, that harmony is achieved through one ingenious compositional effect: the distance between our viewpoint and the train.

Although the distance is not overwhelming, the train is still far enough that it looks small, gentle, and unobtrusive in the midst of the wholeness and sublimity of the landscape. We have, therefore, come to the truth of the matter: there is no "real" equivalence—at least not in the material space devoted to—between the new technology and nature in the "landscape of reconciliation." In fact, a transcendental painting, like *Delaware Water Gap*, depends upon nature's capacity to transcend anything.

Body Of Ideology: Psychoanalysis And Art

Before examining the various themes of interest in *Delaware Water Gap*, I will set forth a Kleinian interpretation of the artistic object and artistic experience, both with respect to the artist and spectator. The conceptual body to follow will provide an all-encompassing theoretical structure for a meta-understanding of *Delaware Water Gap* and the spectatorial experience associated with it. I will primarily focus my attention on two essays by Adrian Stokes: "Painting and the Inner World" and "Form in Art." Without question, Stokes' theory of art which is, in essence, nothing less than a developed model of object-relations theory, is of extreme interest if only because he was a painter, art critic, and art historian. I need to make clear, at once, that I will selectively choose those aspects of his theory that are most general and most applicable to *Delaware Water Gap* and *Lackawanna Valley*.

Object Relations And Art

Stokes starts out with this premise: art, in object-relations theory, must be seen as a privileged means of relating to an object. Far from deriving any simple pleasure from this experience, artist and spectator are deeply entangled in a process which involves a "gradual wearing down" and "feelings of great guilt." For Stokes, any encounter with the canvas involves "supreme difficulty."[25] (We can interject here to say that surely such a theory of encounter with the canvas only ever really applies to the creator and critic. Is it at all likely that a child would experience "supreme difficulty" in its encounter with the art-object?)

Precisely within this "supreme difficulty" can "aesthetic pleasure" be located. For the artist and spectator, aesthetic pleasure resides in "the creating and perceiving of an object whose integrity has been fought for."[26] After one's entanglement with the canvas is complete, "guilt is assuaged rather than circumvented."[27]

As my quotation of Stokes at the very outset of the essay infers, the prototype for the artistic interaction, both in relation to the artist and his medium and the spectator to the art-object, is the unconsciously felt encounter between infant and mother. The medium of production, the artist's medium, is nothing less than the mother's body. The act of creation and the experience thereof, as Elizabeth Wright describes it, involves "the separating out of the bodily self from the primal object."[28]

The creative act, therefore, repeats the primal experience of separation from the mother. (An exciting link exists here between Stokes' object-relations theory of art and Bloom's interpretation of the sublime. "Giving birth to poems," for Bloom, "is to relive the primal anxiety."[29]

Kleinian analysts, according to Wright, have taken Stokes' theory of art a step further. D.W. Winnicott, for example, argues that the creative act can take place in the context of either of these two positions: the "schizoid-paranoid" or the "depressive."[30] The difference between both states is that the schizoid-paranoid artist experiences his objects as fragmented, whereas the depressive experiences them as integrated. In "Form and Art," Stokes regards the depressive position as providing the *mise-en-scène* for artistic creation. The depressive mind, then, is the very factor which conditions the outcome of the form the art-object is to take.

Modern day Kleinians would not disagree, but they would add that the depressive artist will invest his or her canvas with the fantasy appropriate to their continuing stage in desire. The schizoid-paranoid position, in contrast, is a state of swinging oscillation between identification with the breast and separation from it. According to Melanie Klein, it is precisely this position which initiates all objectifications.[31] ("Objective" art, in its denotative and connotative senses, will be a concept of relevance when I turn to Inness' *Lackawanna Valley*.)

In essence, then, Kleinian theory can account for two types of artistic experience, one which can be seen as harmonizing (the depressive) and the other as rebellious. It is crucial to understand, however, that in either case, the unconscious is seen as the investing agency in the form of the art object. The unconscious generation of form occurs through the material interaction of artist and medium.

The weaknesses and strengths of object-relations theory, in relation to art, are made apparent once they are applied to Inness' *Delaware Water Gap*. In many respects, the theory tends to be purely hypothetical. Stokes' notions of a gradual wearing down and of great guilt involved in the artist's relation to the art-object remain psychoanalytic abstractions, especially when applied to *Delaware Water Gap*. Who is to know whether Inness' or the critic's encounter with the art-object will involve gruelling experience and guilt-ridden anxiety. This is, undoubtedly, a question only God can answer.

Another abstraction, or weakness in the theory, is the necessary deduction that the form in *Delaware Water Gap* (and in all art) is determined by the unconscious. According to Stokes, the form in art is always ever produced by the unconscious because the initial stage of creativity invests heavily in a regression to the mother's breast. Such a regression we can safely assume occurs unconsciously.

That is, the very medium, the canvas the artist must fill, is nothing more than a substitute for the mother's breast. One can in turn deduce that the initial experience in art sees the infant/artist returning to the oral stage. Such a theory of art is of metaphorical interest, but can anyone prove, empirically, that the artist's canvas is the mother's breast? Consequently, if the canvas is not a breast, we cannot take for granted the notion that form, in art, is unconsciously determined.

In looking at *Delaware Water Gap* I am inclined, instead, to argue for a reading which lays heavier emphasis on conscious desire (deeply influenced by thoughts of the pastoral, the transcendental, and the sublime) as determining the form in Inness' painting. Is it not explicit that in *Delaware Water Gap*, Inness strives, uncompromisingly, toward a conscious rendering of an ideal and sublime topos? Form and content mingle harmoniously to create a sense of paradisal bliss. Not one trace of a rough spot can be detected in the *Delaware Water Gap*. The excessive and indeed strange luminosity of the painting is again only a conscious symptom/signal of a desire to transcend a world of "accidents" and "mere facts."

Inness, in creating Delaware Water Gap, has fulfilled a conscious wish: the creation of the other-worldly nature of the sublime. Object-relations theory, therefore, can be countered with this thesis: in *Delaware Water Gap* form is consciously produced in order to fulfil a conscious aim which has little to do with "the" mother's breast.

The danger, then, in Stokes' theory of artistic creation is that in its insistence on a return to an oral stage, we are left with a completely unconscious (individually determined) model of understanding the creative act. The model is fraught with a stress on "not knowing" as "a not being aware." The infant, for example, surely does not experience in a rational and coherent manner its attachment to the breast; that is, a child does not have the capacity at its stage in life to consciously realize the pleasure it derives from its first love-object. (Can this be the case with Inness also?)

The most appropriate question following such a deduction would then be: are there any symptoms in *Delaware Water Gap* which indicate, in a concrete manner, a wholly unconscious mode of production? Can we, with any degree of seriousness and fairness, confine Inness to the role of unaware infant? As I have pointed out, *Delaware Water Gap* is symptomatic of a psyche which is consciously aware of its mode of production and in strong control of the themes, the genre, and the desires that govern it. Certainly Cikovsky, Jr. and Marx would agree that Inness is treating both the genre of landscape painting and the social theme of the train in a fully rational manner.

So far I have brought to light what I feel are blindspots in Stokes' theory of artistic experience and creation. I will now turn to the strengths of his theory. Stokes' idea of "supreme difficulty," of pleasure gained only from the creating "of an object whose integrity has been fought for" is sound even though it remains in the realm of hypothesis. (Here it may seem like I am contradicting my earlier criticism of Stokes' concept of a "gradual wearing down" and of "great guilt," but it seems to me that a distinction can be made between feelings of guilt attached to creative activity and the knowledge of the difficulty inherent in the production of art.) One can safely say, for instance, that conflict and struggle are at the base of most art, and this is especially true with respect to the great harmony (correspondence between orders), sublimity, and reconciliation depicted in *Delaware Water Gap*.

Also worth consideration, if read conservatively, is the second half of Stokes' theory of the return to the mother's breast. There Stokes argues that the creative act repeats the primal experience of separating from the mother. I do not see why one should not take such a hypothesis further—for the creation of the creative object, one pre-condition must remain constant: the artist's conscious knowledge that a separation did occur once before, and that it is about to occur once again in the production of creativity.

Finally, the Kleinian splitting of two possible types of artistic experience and consequent creation is of extreme, unquestionable importance to the present study. The distinction Klein and Winnicott make between "depressive" and "schizoid-paranoid" art will permit a strong structural base from which a comparative analysis of *Delaware Water Gap* and *Lackawanna Valley* will be fruitful. Furthermore, although such a frame for an understanding of art is reductive, it nevertheless allows us to gain precious insight into the artist's psyche (a psyche which, in Inness' case, may be shifting in movement from one painting to the next). For now, it will suffice to say that because it is a paradigm of integration and harmony, *Delaware Water Gap* is a creation determined by the "depressive" mode.

The Railroad-In-The-Landscape: *Delaware Water Gap*

Of course "The Railroad-in-the-Landscape" forms part of the title of a truly seminal essay on the subject by Marx. In his essay—before entering into an analysis of Delaware Water Gap—he describes it as a "dreamy, dream-like Hudson River school painting."[32] There is no question the painting is dream-like; everything seems to carry the dream-aesthetic across: from the excessive, paradise-like light to the other-worldly brownish-yellow color which dominates. Even the strangely floating barge which seems to be suspended in air and the incredible stillness of the water add to the atmosphere of dream. Moreover, *Delaware Water Gap* follows very closely the artistic codes of the pastoral mode. It does, for instance, describe a simplicity, peace, and harmony. One can also argue that it has been inscribed with a "yearning for a pre-fall paradisal life in which man exists in harmony with nature."

All this is to permit myself to make a link between pastoral art and dream. In my definition of the pastoral mode, I implicitly uncovered its strong base in dream and desire. I will now make it explicit: the pastoral aesthetic, in its very essence, is always in search of a return to a dream state. (Thus, it is only with respect to the mode that a pastoral painting depicts a kind of dream.) A logical consequence of my formulation, then, would be to closely examine *Delaware Water Gap* as dream. In doing so, I believe a most accurate "coming to terms" with the pastoral mode and Inness' painting will flourish. What is to follow, therefore, is a psychoanalytic dream interpretation of *Delaware Water Gap*. In my analysis, I will rely upon a symbolical reading of the train, the landscape, and the river.

Under Sigmund Freud's symbolic interpretations of dream content, the railroad-in-the-landscape becomes an image of shocking and significant meaning. All innocence is lost once the train and the landscape in *Delaware Water Gap* is placed in the realm of dream, and then held under the psychoanalytic microscope. For one, the train suddenly is to be interpreted as a penetrating phallus. (I add "penetrating" to phallus so that I may stress the train's forward movement in *Delaware Water Gap*.) The landscape, on the other hand, is to be interpreted, initially, as the human body.

In this preliminary and highly superficial stage of interpretation, a specific sex is not assigned to the landscape. Freud's earliest interpretation of the appearance of landscapes in dreams simply states that they come to represent the human body and the genitals:

> Whereas to the innocent eye they appear as plans, maps, and so on, closer inspection shows that they represent the human body, the genitals, etc.[33]

Clearly, such an interpretation of the landscape in dreams remains vague and uncertain. A year after this initial interpretation, in 1912, Freud argues more assuredly and convincingly that "landscapes in dreams, especially any containing bridges or wooded hills, may clearly be recognized as descriptions of the genitals."[34]

Still, a sex has not been assigned. Nevertheless, in Freud's second interpretation an obvious link exists between the interpretation of landscapes in dreams and *Delaware Water Gap*.

A landscape containing wooded hills and a bridge describes to a great extent Inness' painting. (In fact, *Delaware Water Gap* is not only blessed with wooded hills in the background and right middleground, but it also depicts wooded patches in places where the land remains at the level of the river.) Ironically enough, however, it is only Freud's earliest interpretation of landscapes in dreams (1909) that is most complete.

> In some dreams of landscapes or other localities, emphasis is laid in the dream itself on a convinced feeling of having been there once before. These places are invariably the genitals of the dreamer's mother; there is indeed no other place about which one can assert with such conviction that one has been there once before.[35]

Delaware Water Gap is unquestionably a description of one of those types of landscape dreams which have a *déjà-vu* feel to them. We have all been to *Delaware Water Gap* once before. As spectators, we are immediately able to identify with, and to create a connection between the form and content of representation in *Delaware Water Gap* and an ideal image we keep locked in our minds. Regardless of whether the mind has seen the ideal landscape or not, as Freud will argue, it has the everpresent capacity to bring it back to life. The consequence of such a connection is radical: the experience of landscapes such as *Delaware Water Gap* forcibly involve a psychical return to the mother's genitalia.

In a few words, then, under the influence of Freudian dream analysis, the landscape in *Delaware Water Gap* is to be considered a representation of the mother's genitalia; the inevitable consequence of which is that the train symbolically transforms itself into the-phallus-in-the-landscape.

In the dream, the minuscule train has crossed the bridge. It is now moving across the meadowy landscape. The "eventuality" I wish to interpret, at length, is the scene of the train about to enter into a thick field of woods. Of course, the train has come to represent, in a most conservative interpretation, the penetrating phallus. Upon closer inspection, however, one notices that out of the train's spout a streak of puffy white smoke can be traced. This trace of white smoke I will interpret as an analogous metaphor of the ejaculatory moment when white semen is released from the male penis. I will insist, therefore, that the train in *Delaware Water Gap* comes to represent the "ejaculating phallus."

But how is it that the phallus releases semen before it passes, on its left side, the chapel (a symbol of the vagina in dreams, according to Freud[36]), or before it enters into the body of woods (pubic hair[37]) ahead? One answer is in fact simple: the train has experienced a plurality of land (bodies) on its way. Like the patch of thick woods it is about to enter, we can assume it has surely experienced many other similar or different patches in its journey across the mother's body. So long as the phallus continues its forward course, therefore, it remains bound to a state of perpetual ejaculation. The train's ejaculation, and this must be stressed, *occurs* in both the physical and emotional sense: that is, Inness' *Delaware Water Gap* is blessed with sublime and overwhelming land (the latter, especially, in relation to the size of the train). The miniscule train, therefore, can at best be overjoyed that it can have "intercourse" with the greater whole. The "ejaculating phallus" is not, because Inness does not allow it to be, of the conquering variety. Indeed, its very size—the very little space it occupies—renders it suppliant to the larger order of nature.

In an indirect manner, I have answered what is an important question to the interpretation of the scene which is to take place between the train and the woods. Still, the question must be stated explicitly: is the ejaculating phallus about to penetrate and violate nature (the mother's vagina) or is it about to be engulfed back into nature's womb?

The latter is surely the case. The miniscule phallus is about to enter a large expanse of woods which is twice its size. Moreover, a return to the womb of nature is most likely because there is no end in sight: that is, the bushy field of woods seemingly stretches to the very end of the canvas. This quality in the composition convincingly conveys the sense that the ejaculating phallus will be lost, will no longer be in the field of vision once it enters into the mysterious woods. The moment of intercourse between train and woods in *Delaware Water Gap* clearly involves a sense of potential loss. Therefore, the ejaculating phallus has reached the point of return; it is then possible to think of Inness' *Delaware Water Gap* as a paradigm of the Emersonian ideal in art. Emerson's ideal was to have the artist work towards incorporating harmoniously, if not appropriating—as is the case here—the train into the greater transcendental whole of nature. The train, in this instance, in the landscape of reconciliation, only ever becomes transcendental through what I have continued to stress: a profound inequality between it and the "Great Order."

So far, in my analysis, I have interpreted an "eventuality"; that is, what would inevitably occur if *Delaware Water Gap* was a moving picture. I will now examine the "scene" from a considerably different methodological approach. I will examine the scene as it really is depicted: from a standpoint which recognizes the frozen stillness inherent in the representational mode of the painter's medium.

In our recognition of stillness in *Delaware Water Gap*, we are forced to omit the previous notion of the train's consequent experience of a plurality of bodies. Subsequently, we are left, instead, with a static image of a train "experiencing" premature ejaculation, of a phallus releasing semen before its proper or usual time.[38] (I must clarify such an interpretation. If such an interpretation is to stand upright, it will depend upon two factors: the perfect stillness and symbolism of the train and smoke; and their consequent relation as symbolic forms to the closest surroundings: i.e., the woods ahead.) But what are the implications, what could be the socio-historical significance of such a radical reading of the train's presence in *Delaware Water Gap*? To be sure, the idea of prematurity leads us in Marx's direction.

From the very outset of his essay on the railroad in the American landscape, Marx brings to light a crucial theme which is to determine the remainder of his discourse. In question form, Marx's thematic concern is best summed up as follows: how does the nineteenth century author and landscape artist come to represent, in their own distinct modes of expression, a recent social phenomena (the train) within the pre-existing rules and conventions of their genre? In a word, how does one come to represent something new within something old?

The landscape artist, according to Marx, was faced with a particularly difficult task. American landscape art was, after all, firmly committed to the representation of either sublime or beautiful American land. Never, in its history, had it been preoccupied with the representation of technology or social change.[39] How, then, was the idea and reality of train, only then in existence (the passenger railroad first appeared on the American scene in the late 1830s), going to take form in landscape art?

In order to answer the question, Marx applies Erwin Panofsky's "iconological" method of art analysis on a wide variety of American landscape paintings with the railroad theme in them. Although Marx does not clearly say so, we can infer—because of the iconological model he has set forth—that the train is depicted in such manner in most of the nineteenth century landscape paintings so as to indicate that its presence in the landscape is premature.

Its very "tininess" in *Delaware Water Gap* as Marx points out, is symptomatic of the notion that the concept and reality of civilization and technological advance was, at the time, very young and fresh in the collective psyche. Marx wisely argues that in almost all landscapes of reconciliation of the nineteenth century, the train's presence does not betray its infancy in both the social and artistic realms. Hence, Inness' depiction of the train in *Delaware Water Gap* falls under the conscious-collective ideological experience of the new machinery. An experience which remained at a level of prematurity, of "not knowing" what the new technology was exactly. Still, however, the image of the railroad-in-the-landscape had to also be read as a signal of oncoming social and artistic change.[40] With this in mind, I have reached the point where I can bare the fruits of a psychoanalytic/iconological reading of the railroad in *Delaware Water Gap*. The train is depicted in such manner as to convey the very real sense of a seeming paradox: prematurity and future change.

It is due time that I turn my attention to a Freudian interpretation of the river. The elongated semi-S curve of the left side and the straightness of the right bank of the river most convincingly represent the mother's pregnant body. In between the banks is the water in the mother's womb. The water is significantly of a mirroring kind: it reflects both the trees along its edge and the bridge that crosses over it. It is indeed the mirroring effect, the color and size, as well as the shape of the river, that almost lures the spectator to immerse himself, or herself, in it. (Marx similarly points to the "attraction" of the river.) The lure of the river takes on great importance when examined under the microscope of psychoanalysis. To begin with, Freud very clearly states in his *Intertpretation of Dreams* that dreams which have the dreamer diving into mirroring water are to be associated with birth.[41]

Both spectator, as Marx aruges, and Inness, find comfort, easiness, and peace in the river. (It is not unlike the river often described in *The Adventures of Huckleberry Finn*.) Inness, at the time he was painting *Delaware Water Gap*, always found comfort in the representation of rivers such as the one described. This obsession is made clear once one examines comparatively his other two paintings of the *Delaware Water Gap*.

Both were painted within the same year as *Delaware Water Gap* and more significantly, all three paintings uncannily reproduce the same qualities (i.e., mirroring water) and the shape of the mother's pregnant body. Inness, it would seem, then, would gladly dive, metaphorically, into the objective form of the mirroring water. The question remains then whether the same can be said about the spectator, and if so, what is the consequence? In answering the question, I need to first describe *where* the spectator is "positioned" in *Delaware Water Gap*.

The audience's initial field of vision, I will speculate, follows the vista set forth by the pine tree in the middle foreground. It is only a small tree, but it finds itself at the centre of the painting. The spectator's position permits two immediate fields of vision: his/her vision will either sail deep into the ominous distance, or it will be lured straight down into the mirroring mystery of the river.

One of the double lures—the river—then, most definitely places the spectator in a position of wishing to dive into the ideal and the unknown—to dive into (even at the expense of bodily harm) the shiny surface of the river. Of course, the double lure—infinity or the river—only become enticing because they hold potential answers to the unknown and death. (In Greek mythology, the river Styx holds the dead in its lower depths.[42] Similarly, in Hindu mythology, infinity is the "possessor" of the dead and death.[43]) Moreover, a close analysis of the river and distance in *Delaware Water Gap* can only reveal how mysterious they ultimately remain. Who is to know what lies beneath the river's unpenetrable surface, and who knows what lies beyond our grasp?

Both river and distance in *Delaware Water Gap*, therefore, are to be interpreted as "abodes" which possess the unknown. In a word, the ominous distance and the river, which cannot be penetrated or unveiled by the spectator-analyst are those elements in *Delaware Water Gap* that embody, that give meaning to the mythical notion of Eleusinian mysteries. These are the precise mysteries which are "believed to ensure happiness in the future world" by imparting "secret formulas" to be used by each "soul in its passage to the future world."[44]

So it is clear, then, that *Delaware Water Gap* is a painting with "transcendental overtones," but let us now return to the question of spectatorship and identification. If *Delaware Water Gap* is, as I have argued above, a *dream* into which the identifying spectator would gladly dive into, is it not clear that what conditions this wish is the desire to be born again? If, in omitting the distance, the spectator falls headfirst into the alluring river, is it not evident that he or she is in quest of a return to the mother's pregnant body?

To be sure, any kind of "diving" into the painting, but especially a diving into the water of *Delaware Water Gap* on the part of the spectator, is indeed symptomatic of a wish to return some place. That "some place" is in fact the "ideal space of return" once examined in the context of Freud's interpretation of persons dreaming about being in water:

> ...a large number of dreams...having as their content such subjects as passing through narrow spaces or being in water are based upon phantasies of intra-uterine life, of existence in the womb and of the act of birth.[45]

The consequence of spectator identification with the river, therefore, suggests a deep, unconscious wish, on the spectator's part, to return to the womb and to re-experience intra-uterine life. The spectator—like Inness—who finds comfort in representations of the landscape, as in *Delaware Water Gap*, is, unconditionally, in search of a bliss which is, paradoxically, unconscious. The identifying spectator returns to images of the pastoral, and to specific forms of the genre (i.e., the river) as Inness does, always in an attempt to fulfill the unconscious wish of a return to an easier, simpler, and accident-free way of life. In light of the above, it is simple to see the definite "interconnectedness" between the pastoral mode and the Bloomian sublime: both forms of desire reveal a singular quest for "lost origins."

Self-Reflexivity And The Theme Of The Double

If *Delaware Water Gap* is an artefact of transcendental art, as Cikovsky, Jr. and Marx argue, it is of imperative value to analyze the nature of its Transcendentalism and the role of the artist within it. In *Delaware Water Gap*, as I have argued before, everything assumes transcendental status: train, river, reapers, etc. It is precisely such a *union* of forces that render a painting transcendental. Within the transcendental wholeness defined in *Delaware Water Gap*, we need to make room for an analysis of the material activity and thematic concern of the "transcendental artist."

In George Inness' *The Lackawanna Valley: Type of the Modern*, Cikovsky, Jr. ingeniously argues that the artist's function in *Delaware Water Gap* is not unlike that of the reapers and the trains in the same painting:

> Civilized landscape, nature shaped by creative intelligence, was thus the counterpart of Inness' modern, indeed, modernist determination, to transform nature into art, to impress his artistic will on nature and use its materials for his own artistic purposes, just as reapers and shepherdesses, woodcutters and surveyors, and of course, railroad builders, used and remade nature according to human design.[46]

The creative and material act of painting *Delaware Water Gap* (of transforrning nature), as Cikovsky, Jr. argues, mimics the activity of the reapers and the trains in the representation. In his essay on the topic, Marx pushes the argument a step further by implying that all three—artist, train, and field workers—are engaged in complicitous, progressive activity. It is quite clear that both reapers and train, forge ahead, in duplicitous manner and direction, towards the west. The train (technological invention) and the reapers (human activity) are the apparent forces and emblems that reveal the modern and rapid reality of expansionism in America.

In depicting the social reality of his time, Inness is also engaged in the work of expansion. Inness, like the train and the reapers, is in the process (ideological) of "forging the west" through the representation of precisely such subject matter. The role of the artist within *Delaware Water Gap's* grounded transcendentalism (a Transcendentalism deeply based in "materiality"), therefore, is to be progressive. In being progressive, Inness, a lot like Asher B. Durand in *Progress* (a painting similar in subject and theme) uncannily and invisibly makes his presence felt in the Transcendental wholeness of the painting. This uncanny aura which surrounds *Delaware Water Gap* is indeed the quality that makes it a representation of the transcendental sublime.

To be sure, part of the reason *Delaware Water Gap* can be interpreted as a sublime painting is due to its perfect harmony—the sublime fusion of external, internal, and invisible forces. Sublimity, therefore, is achieved through the perfect adaptation of spirituality in matter, and the uncanny fusion of God, nature, man) and the artist. In a word, Inness creates sublimity through his systematic and faithful translation of transcendental philosophy. (Another possible hypothesis is that Inness may, in fact, have produced sublimity by pushing transcendental doctrine to its extreme.)

One aspect of the sublime in *Delaware Water Gap* has been analysed; what still remains unclear, however, is an understanding of Inness' progressive attitude and its relation to transcendental philosophy. Another key issue that requires examination is the artwork's strong social base.

Cikovsky, Jr. presents to us an image of Inness as "the first *modernist*" in American landscape painting; similarly, Marx paints a portrait of Inness as progressive man. In either case, Inness is, under the influence of Emersonian language, a "transcendentalist." If, as Emerson said, "Machinery and Transcendentalism agree well because Stage Coach and Railroad are bursting the old legislation like green withes," then it can also be said that Inness and Transcendentalism agree well because he is representative of the progressive process that is concerned with disrupting the old, worn-out conventions of the landscape form by representing the new, changing reality of the machine in its midst.

In its essence, Transcendentalism was a highly progressive discourse, and Inness in turn was a highly progressive artist, just as the train was, in turn, a technological reality signifying both change and progress. Therefore, if the railroad system functioned as "revolution" in reality, Inness' *Delaware Water Gap* functions as revolution at the creative level.[47] Both Inness' art and the train, then, were representative of dynamic new forces directed against old conventions and forms of thought and behaviour.[48]

Finally, any labelling of *Delaware Water Gap* as a painting grounded by a social materialism must be clarified. *Delaware Water Gap* simultaneously transcends mere fact, mere matter, and is, paradoxically enough, grounded by it because it depicts a material truth of great significance: the emergence of the railroad in the American landscape.

The theme of the double and self-reflexivity operate within a single structural rubric of interpretation in *Delaware Water Gap*. The representation of Inness' double is, in a word, a self-reflexive act. Although I have already hinted at, or made implicit, the notion of "doubling" in Inness' painting, I will here try to deconstruct the appearance of a doubling effect and the artist's psychical experience accompanying such representation.

As I argued above, a transcendental (mystical, uncanny) correlation exists between artist, man, and machinery. Both man and machine are internal projections of Inness' psyche which find concrete expression in the body of the canvas; therefore, they are nothing but displaced and ideational doubles of the artist. The reapers and the train, however, are not disconnected doubles. That is, one does not describe something wholly different from the other; instead, reapers and train, especially in relation to purpose, mimic each other perfectly. Within *Delaware Water Gap*, therefore, the train and the reapers are rendered in such manner as to indicate an obverse doubling between man and technology. But what is the process through which the train—a technological and seemingly separate entity—becomes a double of man? Barbara Novak offers a psychological insight in her section on trains in *Nature and Culture* that responds well to the question.

According to Novak, through a process of introjection—"a process whereby qualities that belong to an external object are absorbed and unconsciously regarded as belonging to the self"[49]— the mid-nineteenth century ego is influenced by both the image and qualities associated with the train. Novak provocatively argues that with the appearance of the train, a mental transformation takes place: the "faculties of mind" suddenly become "mathematical" and engineer-oriented.[50] The train, therefore, becomes an extended double of man through a process of "technologization of mind." And the appearance of the technological double transpires through the subsequent projection into art and literature of the technological mind.

Such a notion is not altogether new, either, for as Paul Coates explains in *The Double and the Other*, "the link between the double and the machine is first made by E.T.A. Hoffmann."[51] Consequently, the machine has had considerable time between *The Sandman* (1819) and *Delaware Water Gap* (1857) to make its impression on the mind. All this is to say that the train as the double of man is indeed a plausibility (just as the robot as man's double is), and its appearance occurs through an elaborate process of introjection and projection. The train in *Delaware Water Gap* is, then, Inness' technological double. Like the reapers, it duplicates the progressiveness which characterizes Inness' art. Upon closer scrutiny, the reapers reveal themselves to be in near affiliation with Inness. They, like the artist, use a tool for the purpose of designing nature. In all fairness, then, the reapers are *closer* to Inness than the train because they reflect his activity more accurately. To be sure, the reapers' progress is closer to the artist's in the literal spatial sense also.

Whereas the train is very small and in the distant background, the reapers are in much closer proximity: only a few inches away from Inness and the spectator. (Of course this is true only if we can delude ourselves into thinking the canvas is not flat.) The positioning of train and reapers in *Delaware Water Gap* is of great interest in that it points to the possible area in which Inness would like to position himself. It is clear within the compositional framework that complicity is suggested between the train and reapers. If a connecting line is drawn between the train and reapers, it is easy to see that the latter have been positioned closer to the west. If, as a starting point, we take the reaper's position and a similar line is projected forward, it eventually finds an end at the lower left hand corner of the painting. This invisible line connects the train and reapers with Inness' position. His position is a little more west than that of the reapers. Inness is at the very edge, at the very vanguard of progress.

At this point, I will return to the theme of the double and its link to self-reflexivity. An outgrowth of the above link will be the idea of *Delaware Water Gap* as mirror. For now, it will suffice to show the triplicate structure of projection and doubling:

A. *The projecting subject—* (Inness)	B. *Objects of projection—* and doubles: The Reapers	C. *Objects of a double* projection system and therefore, a double of a double: The Train

A triple 'I' ('I' for Inness), therefore, can be arguably located in *Delaware Water Gap*: 'I' in the reapers, 'I' in the train, and 'I' in the whole. 'I' transcends the limits of mere representation and, as a consequence, appears everywhere within the *Delaware Water Gap* landscape. It is within such a frame of interpretation that *Delaware Water Gap* comes to be seen as a self-reflexive painting. (An inversion of the projection model also reveals the self-reflexive nature of the painting. Instead of beginning with Inness, we are left with Inness. The painting suddenly becomes, through inverted reduction, nothing other than Inness.) In addition, *Delaware Water Gap* is self-reflexive due to the projection of doubles which are, in their essence, extensions of the artist's progressive psychical disposition.

It is clear, then, that Inness' painting is a mirror which reflects an image of its creator's thoughts. The canvas in this instance, and in all instances, has indirectly absorbed the artist's ego by seducing it onto its very own surface. *Delaware Water Gap* is, then, an image of Inness' mental structure and therefore its function is that of a mirror: it is eternally ready for Inness' and the progressive spectator's narcissistic looking—it is a mirror made for the grand purpose of mirroring.

The Lackawanna Valley

The Impressive Tree: It is located in the left foreground of *The Lackawanna Valley*. Further to the left is the train track. Beneath it and slightly to the right is the solitary shepherd-like figure reclining comfortably. The impressive tree is the strongest vertical element in the painting. It reaches way up into *The Lackawanna Valley* sky and almost succeeds in establishing contact with the uppermost left corner of the canvas. This birch tree is part of both worlds: its existence is both tied to the concrete base of the ground and the infinite realm of the sky. Interestingly enough, this tree is almost as solitary as the shepherd: it is one of two trees that have survived the cutting and slashing of the civilizing project. The patches of light and dark bark are sure signs of the type of tree (birch) it is. The impressive tree's slim silhouette, height,and fullness make it a graceful representation of powerful beauty.

The Shepherd: The pastoral figure in the left foreground conveys a sense of tranquil calm. As the shepherd reclines and contemplates the coming of the train, it is easy to see that he has not accidentally chosen his spot. The cleared path which leads precisely to the shepherd seems to indicate that this is a very popular location indeed. The shepherd has his back turned to us and is wearing a white straw hat, a red pullover, a white shirt, and grey pants. (The overall effect is that of a person from the country.) His vision is directed towards the emerging train.

In his immediate field of vision, a field of green grass with tell-tale stumps is visible. Behind him, in the very foreground, the four evident stumps are not quite as ugly or as telling of the tragic conquest of civilization over nature as the ones before him. The two stumps in the central foreground and the other to the extreme left foreground are depicted in such manner so as to remain, because of their detail, interesting and not aesthetically impoverished. The field of stumps before the shepherd, however, conveys an unhomely, unnatural sense of imperfections growing out of the ground.

The Train And Its Surroundings: Barbara Novak says that the train in *Lackawanna Valley* is the "main protagonist." To be sure, it occupies more space than the *Delaware Water Gap* train (in the middleground), and, because of its positioning, it draws our immediate attention. But what is most unusual and exciting about the *Lackawanna Valley* train is its seemingly human face. Upon closer scrutiny, the front end of the locomotive betrays a semblance of a human beard of the type often associated with the old English guard or aristocrat.

This impressive train is unquestionably depicted in such a manner as to render it gentle and humane. There is nothing rough about its look. The train, in itself, therefore, does not carry the impression that it is the potential cause of the destruction or conquering of nature. This is also emphasized by the cottony puffs of smoke that rise out of its engines. Having chosen the right track instead of the left, the *Lackawanna Valley* train is, a lot like its *Dela-*

ware Water Gap counterpart, heading west. Both tracks in the center-middleground, enveloped by an intricate fencing structure, lead off into opposite directions. One is left to wonder whether the railroad system has by now left a permanent trace from the east to the westernmost point of the new land. The fence and tracks inevitably also function as emblems of an existing difference between technology and nature.

Of the twenty-two cars following the train, the second one is of particular interest. It is carrying lumber, and on the left side, written in bold yet imprecise letters, is the company's name (D.L. & W.R.). One can safely assume that at least several of the many cars were used for the transportation of passengers. The locomotive seems to have made its way out of the roundhouse.

The impressive train is, without doubt, in the midst of a peculiar natural environment. To the left, where the field has been cleared, four cows are scattered amidst anomalous stumps and a single bush. The single cypress tree, close to the track, along with the lonely bush amidst the cleared field are tell-tale signs—and sad ones at that—of the defacement of nature. Nevertheless, the cypress tree on the right side of the track and the birch tree on the left remain upright and strong.

On both sides of the middleground, from which the train is emerging, complete and untouched patches of nature remain. In the left middleground, especially, a variety of tall and graceful trees can be seen. These trees, complete with reclining figure, most surely symbolize the pastoral mode.

The Town: John F. Kasson says of the town: "the industrial buildings in the background nestle gently between the far hills and the groves of trees in the middle distance."[52] The industrial town in *Lackawanna Valley* contains the following: a chapel; a roundhouse; town houses; factory buildings; and one long, extending central street.

With the help of a magnifying glass, one can detect at least six inhabitants in Inness' little town. There are four alternate railroad tracks and three other almost insignificant (in relation to size) trains expelling white smoke around the central part of the town. Smoke is, indeed, everywhere to be seen: white, puffy smoke a lot like that of the trains, arises from the chapel, the factory buildings, and the roundhouse.

Strangely enough, the cottony puffs that rise from the buildings of secular invention (roundhouse, factories) duplicate the puff that rises from behind the church. This seems to suggest a mysterious correspondence between the secular and the spiritual. An evident color contrast exists between the foreground space of the painting and the town; the affecting contrast between the surrounding green vegetation and the arid yellow-brownishness of the town's industrial space suggests that a slight difference might exist between nature and civilization. A layer of smoke hovers above the little town.

The Hills And Sky: The smoky haze hovering over the yard reaches back towards the hills (or is it just morning fog settling atop the hills?). Even the hills, which add to the pastoral calm of the painting, have been infected by the ugly pollutants of civilization. These hills are uneven, and of a pinkish-grey color. Above, the sky—taking up one quarter of the composition—is of a gentle blue tint.

Complex Pastoralism, Roughness, And Rudeness

In comparison to *Delaware Water Gap*, *Lackawanna Valley* is very different in all of these three areas: style, mode, and signification. A look at what Marx, Cikovsky, Jr., and Novak have to say about the painting will shed light on this difference. To begin with, Cikovsky, Jr., in comparing *Lackawanna Valley*'s style to the other two *Delaware Water Gap* paintings, writes:

> In *The Lackawanna Valley*, the handling is broader, more painterly, and the contrasts of value and hue are more emphatic than in the other two, which are painted with a delicacy of color and a meticulous, controlled handling and attention to detail.[53]

Cikovsky, Jr., goes on to say that,

> ...if the paintings are a set, there was at some point and for some reason a sudden change in Inness' style.[54]

Indeed, a change in style did take place between Delaware Water Gap and *Lackawanna Valley*: the brushwork in the latter is considerably less precise, but nevertheless, I would caution against a reductive reading which insists that the style is simply suggestive, allusive, and subjective. In my description of the train in *Lackawanna Valley* for example, I was able to focus on a very high degree of detail. It is, therefore, fair to say, with caution, that Inness' style in *Lackawanna Valley* is generally, but not fully, suggestive in breadth and energetic in the handling of the subject matter.

Marx's interpretation of style in *Lackawanna Valley* remains vague within the framework of his simple statement that "it is not a dreamy Hudson River style painting."[55] Nevertheless, in his attempt to find "a mode of painting," a descriptive frame in which to place *Lackawanna Valley*, his notion of "complex pastoralism" is most satisfactory.

According to Marx, *Lackawanna Valley* exemplifies what he argues is a more complex version of the pastoral. There has been an evolution in his interpretation of the *Lackawanna Valley*. In *The Machine in the Garden*, Marx simply defines Inness' painting as "a more industrialized version of the pastoral ideal." As a landscape style or mode, complex pastoralism is distinguished by the presence of a quite different and less easily assimilated set of images: patches of unruly, wild vegetation; the jagged stumps of recently felled trees; unsightly clearings in the forest; the dark smoke of locomotives filling the sky, or the glare of their headlights penetrating the dark; fleeing, frightened animals; Native Americans, sometimes in defiant or menacing postures, sometimes in melancholy retreat before the forward march of white European civilization.[56]

Although many of the latter discordant images described by Marx are more applicable to Asher B. Durand's *Progress*, the first four can be directly applied to Inness' *Lackawanna Valley*. Wild vegetation, stumps, unsightly or unnatural clearings, and a formation of smoke filling the atmosphere are all part of the *Lackawanna* reality. Cikovsky, Jr., in contrast, only slightly modifies, in order to fit in Inness' *Lackawanna Valley*, his original category of the "civilized landscape" mode. The *Lackawanna Valley* according to Cikovsky, is simply a more explicit and frank expression of a subject matter that had always preoccupied Inness' art:

> *The Lackawanna Valley*, therefore, is only a more explicit and forceful rendering of the kind of civilized subject Inness depicted in a succession of paintings.[57]

It is of interest to note that Cikovksy, Jr. uses obsessively "unequivocal frankness" in his interpretation of the painting. Novak, on the other hand, cannot place *Lackawanna Valley* within the idealism of the pastoral mode because its "forcefulness" and "documentary look" render it "shocking": "Yet some of the shock of this picture—and it is, I think, a shocking picture—is due to the fact that the pastoral idea has been so rudely treated."[58] The *Lackawanna Valley* in Novak's view—Marx and Cikovsky, Jr. do not disagree—needs to be discussed within the frame of a "picture" and not a painting. It is a picture, according to Novak, which is fraught with a "rude realism." For Marx, Cikovsky Jr. and Novak, a very definite shift has taken place between the *Lackawanna Valley* and *Delaware Water Gap*: the latter is a painting, and an ideal one at that, of the existing socio-historical scene, whereas the former is better understood as a picture of such a scene.

Novak, especially, finds Inness' *Lackawanna Valley* a very difficult picture to interpret. Towards the end of her last paragraph in *Nature and Culture*, a sense of postmodern indeterminacy is conveyed:

> The picture's interpretation remains open, and it is impossible to read it 'correctly.' It is a singular and somewhat mysterious picture. It underlines the dangers of reading 'intention,' particularly when our attitudes to the machine and nature have suffered such radical alterations.[59]

Novak's criticism surely remains at a too simple and general level. But she nevertheless points to the definite danger of trying to read Inness' complex painting in a positivist manner. Although Cikovsky, Jr. agrees that there is no "correct" reading of *Lackawanna Valley*, he is much more optimistic about the picture's meaning: "It is not quite as elusive, as mysterious, as Novak says, nor as relative to changing tastes and times."[60] For Cikovsky, Jr., *Lackawanna Valley* can be interpreted because of its "roughness of style and meaning." Cikovsky, Jr.'s interpretation is unambiguous and optimistic:

> What is more, the unequivocal frankness with which he depicted the railroad's encounter with nature in the *Lackawanna Valley*, the warmth and brightness of the paintings light and the clarity of its atmosphere, forbid insinuations of doubt or irony or criticism.[61]

Such an easy interpretation of *Lackawanna Valley* is not altogether unproblematic. Although there is a great degree of frankness in *Lackawanna Valley*, it is not a painting of "unequivocal frankness." Inness' depiction of the train is much more gentle and personal than its real life counterpart. In *Lackawanna Valley*, as in *Delaware Water Gap*, Inness has tried to represent the great locomotive in such manner so as to please his commissioners—the Delaware, Lackawanna and Western Railroad Company. Furthermore, it is extremely difficult to "concretize" Cikovsky, Jr.'s claims of "warmth, brightness of light, and clarity of atmosphere" in *Lackawanna Valley*. The latter claim is especially open to debate (most critics have suggested the opposite regarding the *Lackawanna* atmosphere). If Cikovsky, Jr.'s initial interpretations of *Lackawanna Valley* are "doubtful," then his consequent and final claim of it being a painting that "forbids insinuations of doubt or irony or criticism" is absurd. In short, Novak's *laissez-faire* criticism, that is, her quick treatment of indeterminacy and Cikovsky, Jr.'s foolhardy optimism are insufficient and inadequate models to work with.

In a rush to open new critical ground, Cikovsky, Jr. in *Type of the Modern* sees too much and too little in his otherwise refreshing analysis of the *Lackawanna Valley*. Cikovsky, Jr. omits any reference to the prominent presence of the locomotive—more conspicuous than the sole surviving group of trees in the middleground—and the unhomely stumps in the foreground. These "omissions" along with the lonely depiction of the cypress tree and the bush in the cleared fields to the left of the train lead me to suspect some ambiguity in Inness' attitude toward the material progress he was asked to paint.

Lackawanna Valley is not, as Cikovsky, Jr. might want to envision it, a conventional landscape of reconciliation. It is, as Marx has made clear, a complex work of art deeply embedded in conflict and ambiguity. *Lackawanna Valley* is, in Marx's view a complex painting because "the conflict it sets forth (between nature and the machine) is so pervasive, so deeply felt, and the contending forces so evenly matched."[62] We can deduce that such conflict—and indeed it is the case—can only situate the spectator in a critical position of judgment where he or she is torn between "two compelling but antithetical ways of interpreting the painting."[63]

It is precisely this equality between the forces of civilization and nature in *Lackawanna Valley* that need to be foregrounded in any interpretation of the painting. The consequence of conflict due to equality in *Lackawanna Valley*, according to Marx, is symptomatic of Inness' deep moral ambiguity about material progress. (For Marx, at the core of Inness' painting is an ineluctable mix of the constructive and the destructive. The outcome of such a profound mix of opposites—of an image bipolar in nature—is the evocation of an "unresolvable ambivalence."[64] Inness' *Lackawanna Valley*, therefore, brings to the fore the hauntingly equivocal and ambiguous signification of the complex clash of the natural and technological worlds.

Body Of Ideology: Transcending The Code, Ambiguity In Art

Of the three "frames of reference" (pastoral mode; Transcendentalism; and the Sublime) used in interpreting *Delaware Water Gap*, only one—the pastoral mode—will be of use in my analysis of *Lackawanna Valley*.

Inness' latter painting has no easy connection to the Bloomian sublime; nor does it have the transcendental overtones of its more harmonious brother. It is, however, possible to examine the progressive nature of the transcendental train, and this in relation to self-reference in *Lackawanna Valley*, but I will choose not to because it is not the most crucial issue to tackle. It will suffice to say that the locomotive in *Lackawanna Valley* is an even more flagrant example of the projection of artist—hence its human look—onto the canvas. In my analysis of *Lackawanna Valley*, I will, however, focus some attention on Stokes' theories of artistic experience and creation. Stokes' distinction between types of artistic creation will reveal, once applied to *Lackawanna Valley*, the psychical difference involved between it and *Delaware Water Gap*. Inness will emerge as an artist capable of producing at least two types of art. Finally, I will focus most of my energies on applying a semiotic analysis of ambiguity to Inness' masterwork.

In *Structuralism and Semiotics*, Terence Hawkes uses Umberto Eco's theoretical writings to explain the existence of ambiguity in art. I will only relate here what I think are the most crucial concepts from a semiotic standpoint on ambiguity. To begin with, Eco's initial argument is that signifiers, when put to aesthetic use, manifest, unconditionally, a high degree of "plurality," or what is otherwise known as ambiguity. Ambiguity is and involves a "mode" of violating the rules of a given code. (*Lackawanna Valley* is, for instance, a glaring example of organized violence committed against the pastoral mode.) Furthermore, ambiguity in art appears to be a way of linking separate "messages" together. An example of this would be the simultaneous existence of a code of pastoral idealism and a code of technological or social threat; the two antithetical codes inevitably claw away at each other, and eventually cause a residue of sense.

According to Eco, the general effect of linking separate "messages," or codes, is the creation, or more precisely, the generation of an "aesthetic idiolect." This "idiolect" induces in the spectator a sense of "cosmicity": that is a feeling of endllessly moving beyond each established level of meaning the moment it is established, of continually transforming its denotations into connotations.[65] The end result of the existence of ambiguity in art is that the spectator can never arrive at a final decoding because of its ceaselessly moving nature.

Towards A Semiotic And Psychoanalytic Interpretation Of *The Lackawanna Valley*

As Marx argues, *Lackawanna Valley* is a classic example of the existence of ambiguity in art. In every respect it seems todescribe and convey Eco's argument:

> He (Eco) seems to be suggesting that the aesthetic message operates as a continuing multi-order system of signification which moves from level to

level, its denotations becoming connotations in a kind of infinite progression.[66]

Lackawanna Valley is full of "disjunctive signifiers" that are very rich in connotative meaning: on the pastoral side is the "impressive tree," the shepherd, and the graceful trees in the middleground; on the social side is the locomotive, the cleared field with stumps, and the industrial setting of the town. These obvious conflicting forces clash continually throughout Lackawanna Valley thus causing its meaning to shift form—eternally.

Indeed, there are even more minute elements in the painting which generate an "aesthetic idiolect." The calmness about the cows in the left middleground, the singular bush, and the cypress tree in the midst of civil onslaught, and the smoky haze over the town are significant, antithetical denotative signifiers which, when interpreted, transform into objects of high connotative value. In the process of attaining high connotative meaning, these conflicating signifiers begin a never-ending battle, the outcome of which is that interpretation of the painting remains fixed in a state of unresolved suspension and ambiguity.

The result, therefore, of the "multi-order" nature of the painting (caused by the bringing together of separate, "disjunctive" messages within the same space) is a crisis of representation and meaning. That is, in the end of the interpretive process we are not quite sure as to how *Lackawanna Valley* should be read, even though everything is represented in intelligible manner. *Lackawanna Valley*, or the "ambiguous artwork," prefigures, therefore, in a strong manner, the post-modernist notion of the "multiple discourse," or as Frederic Jameson would name it, "schizophrenicity." (When each signifier in *Lackawanna Val-*

ley is brought into discourse with its perfect opposite—its monstrous other—it begins to speak a multi-layered language that is impossible to control.) In sum, it is clear that in *Lackawanna Valley* Inness has transcended the limits of the pastoral code through his creative reorganization and interpretation of the code. *The Lackawanna Valley* in a truly direct way, can be thought of as a more ambiguous version of the socio-pastoral mode.

Lackawanna Valley, is, as we have seen, a painting entangled in ambiguity. This quality makes it one of the most revolutionary paintings of mid-nineteenth century America. But, a fundamental question remains unanswered: Does *Lackawanna Valley* really reveal, as Marx argues, Inness' "deep moral ambivalence about material progress?" Clearly the gruesome tell-tale stumps inevasibly transmit a sense of doubt and ambivalence on the past of the author. Moreover, the smoky haze enveloping the town and hills is of foreboding character. Nevertheless, the train itself does not reveal, as Marx would have it, signs which could be read as Inness' ambivalence towards "material progress." From the detailed depiction of the locomotive, one can only infer that Inness himself is in affinity with the spirit and purpose of the locomotive.

Even this last formulation is countered, however, by the train's overwhelmingly prominent presence. And this leads us to the very nature of the painting: two contending forces—nature and civilization, or good and evil—in *Lackawanna Valley* have been so well matched that even a careful statement, such as Marx's, is irreparably incorrect.

What can be said with certainty, *per contra*, about Inness' painting is that it is a radical depiction of a whole new way of life. The huge roundhouse, the industrially organized town, and the emerging spark of the train are glaring symptoms of a completely new economic and social organization. That is, the complete depiction of the railroad system—from roundhouse to tracks to locomotives—is emblematic, reflective of the exact "change" that is taking effect in mid-nineteenth century America.

Inness' *Lackawanna Valley* is, therefore, a great classic of American painting because it captures, realistically, the transitional period it was created in. And if ambivalence is so deeply engrained in the painting, part of the reason, it would seem, is that transition was only then (1850s) taking place. *Lackawanna Valley* magnificently describes the mental attitude of a nation experiencing change.

In the first part of this essay, using Adrian Stokes' Kleinian influenced theory, I explained and explored the two possible positions from which the genesis of art evolves. In "Depressive" art, the artist experiences his objects as "integrated" and the final product of such art can be described as "harmonious." *Delaware Water Gap* is paradigmatic, as was shown, of art having integrated objects and a harmony about it. Since *Lackawanna Valley* is a different "picture," Stokes' theory must account for an alternate position and explanation. To be sure, *Lackawanna Valley* is to be understood as a "schizoid-paranoid" creation within the framework of object-relations ideology. In contrast to the "Depressive" mode, the "schizoid-paranoid" artist experiences his objects as "fragmented," and the end product is "rebellious."

Although Stokes' theoretical model is reductive, it is consummate in its application to both paintings. Inness' *Lackawanna Valley* is indeed rich in fragmented objects. The cows, the cypress tree, the stumps and bush especially, seem to be nothing other than dislocated objects projected onto a more complete whole. In its very essence, the *Lackawanna Valley* describes, profoundly, a disjunctive contest between fragments. (The impressive tree, emblematic of nature, fights off the emergent spirit of the locomotive, which is emblematic of civilization. Such contests, ending without a winner, are staged throughout.)

Hence, the inevitable impression that Inness' *Lackawanna Valley* may have post-modernist roots sprouting in its most remote parts. That is, some of the objects in *Lackawanna Valley*—the cows and the bush—seem to suggest a separate and disinterested existence: their purpose and meaning is minimal, whereas their "objectification" or fragmentation from the whole, is great. *Lackawanna Valley* is, moreover, a work of "schizoid-paranoid" character because its conduct towards the pastoral code is "rebellious." If the pastoral mode has not been "treated rudely," then it has at least been treated creatively. In either case, the end result is a rebellion or violence against, or a transcendence of the code of conduct.

Finally, it is very appropriate, indeed, that the "schizoid-paranoid" position should be the one that "initiates" all "objectifications in art." Whereas *Delaware Water Gap* is a "Depressive" work of art, *Lackawanna Valley* is "objective"—in terms of form and realism—and is, therefore, a "schizoid-paranoid" creation.

Notes

1. It is unfair to use "delusive" in relation to positivist discourse. It is true that at times certainty or positive discourses overlook the fundamental complexity of their objects of study, but it is nevertheless false to argue that they are more prone to delusion than relativist discourses.
2. J.A., Cuddon, *A Dictionary of Literary Terms* (London: Andre Deutsch, 1977), p. 477.
3. Cuddon, *A Dictionary of Literary Terms*, p. 478.
4. Cuddon, *A Dictionary of Literary Terms*, p. 479.
5. Cuddon, *A Dictionary of Literary Terms*, p. 479.
6. Cuddon, *A Dictionary of Literary Terms*, p. 481.
7. Christopher Norris, *Deconstruction: Theory and Practice* (London: Methuen, 1982), p. 141.
8. Barbara Novak, *Nature and Culture: American Landscape and Painting* (New York: Oxford UP, 1980), p. 29, 271, 272.
9. Novak, *Nature and Culture*, p. 271.
10. Leo Marx, "The Railroad-in-the-Landscape: An Iconological Reading of a Theme in American Art," in *The Railroad in American Art: Representations of Technological Change*, eds., Susan Danly and Leo Marx (Cambridge, MA: M.I.T. Press, 1988), p. 199.
11. Marx, "The Railroad-in-the-Landscape," p. 200.
12. The definition of the word barge is to be found in *The Concise Oxford Dictionary*, ed., R.E. Allen (Oxford: Oxford University Press, 1990), p. 87.
13. Nicolai Cikovsky, Jr., "George Inness' *The Lackawanna Valley*," in *The Railroad in American Art: Representations of Technological Change*, eds., Susan Danly and Leo Marx (Cambridge, MA: M.I.T. Press, 1988), p. 83.
14. Cikovsky, "George Inness' *The Lackawanna Valley*," p. 83.
15. Marx, "The Railroad-in-the-Landscape," p. 198.
16. Marx, "The Railroad-in-the-Landscape," p. 199.
17. Marx, "The Railroad-in-the-Landscape," p. 200.
18. Kenneth Clark, *Landscape into Art* (New York: Harper and Row, 1976), p. 6.
19. Clark, *Landscape into Art*, p. 7.
20. Both Nicolai Cikovsky and Leo Marx agree on this point. It does not seem in any way likely that an argument contradicting the perfect harmony of technology and nature in *Delaware Water Gap* could stand.
21. Cikovsky, "George Inness' *The Lackawanna Valley*," p. 87.
22. "The Railroad-in-the-Landscape," p. 205.

23. "The Railroad-in-the-Landscape," p. 198.

24. "The Railroad-in-the-Landscape," p. 199.

25. Stokes' theory is taken from Elizabeth Wright's *Psychoanalytic Criticism: Theory in Practice* (New York: Methuen, 1984), p. 84.

26. Wright, *Psychoanalytic Criticism*, p. 84.

27. Wright, *Psychoanalytic Criticism*, p. 84.

28. *Psychoanalytic Criticism*, p. 84.

29. *Psychoanalytic Criticism*, p. 153.

30. *Psychoanalytic Criticism*, p. 84 - 85.

31. Wright, *Psychoanalytic Criticism*, p. 84.

32. Marx, "The Railroad-in-the-Landscape," p. 200.

33. Sigmund Freud, *The Interpretation of Dreams*, trans. James Strachey (New York: Penguin, 1985), p. 474.

34. Freud, *The Interpretation of Dreams*, p. 473.

35. Freud, *The Interpretation of Dreams*, p. 524.

36. Freud, *The Interpretation of Dreams*, p. 485.

37. Freud, *The Interpretation of Dreams*, p. 485.

38. It is of interest to analyse *Delaware Water Gap* as both still painting and moving picture. Its very subject matter allows one the opportunity to do so. It does not follow however that one is conflating painting and cinema by examining *Delaware Water Gap* in such a manner. Painting and cinema are forms of representation, but they are ultimately very different in nature. See the work of Roger Scruton and Gregory Currie for illuminating distinctions between the cinematic and artistic image.

39. Marx, "The Railroad-in-the-Landscape," p. 203 - 206.

40. See, once again, the latter part of Marx's "The Railroad-in-the-Landscape" for a comprehensive analysis of the technological factors which determined social and artistic change in nineteenth century America.

41. Freud, *The Interpretation of Dreams*, p. 524.

42. J.E. Zimmerman, *Dictionary of Classical Mythology* (New York: Bantam, 1985) p. 249.

43. *Hindu Myths: A Sourcebook*, trans. Wendy Doniger O'Flaherty (Baltimore: Penguin, 1975), p. 303.

44. Zimmerman, *Dictionary of Classical Mythology*, p. 93.

45. Freud, *The Interpretation of Dreams*, p. 524.
46. Cikovsky, "George Inness' *The Lackawanna Valley*," p. 87.
47. Marx, "The Railroad-in-the-Landscape," p. 204 - 205.
48. Marx, "The Railroad-in-the-Landscape," p. 205.
49. The definition of introjection is taken from Elizabeth Wright's *Psychoanalytic Criticism: Theory in Practice*, p. 80.
50. Barbara Novak, *Nature and Culture: American Landscape and Painting*, p. 159 - 161.
51. Paul Coates analyses the various forms the double can have in literature and art in *The Double and the Other: Identity as Ideology in Post-Romantic Fiction* (New York: St. Martin's Press, 1988), p. 3 - 8.
52. John F. Kasson, *Civilizing the Machine: Technology and Republican Values in America, 1776 - 1900* (New York: Grossman, 1976), p. 33.
53. Cikovsky, "George Inness' *The Lackawanna Valley*," p. 87.
54. This essentially translates to—for Cikovsky, Jr.—a "roughness of style" in *Lackawanna Valley* which is not found in the other two paintings.
55. Marx, "The Railroad-in-the-Landscape," p. 204, 205.
56. Marc, "The Railroad-in-the-Landscape," p. 204.
57. Cikovsky, "George Inness' *The Lackawanna Valley*," p. 87.
58. Barbara Novak, *Nature and Culture: American Landscape and Painting*, p. 172.
59. Novak, *Nature and Culture*, p. 174.
60. Cikovsky, "George Inness's *The Lackawanna Valley*," p. 83.
61. Cikovsky, "George Inness's *The Lackawanna Valley*," p. 83.
62. Marx, "The Railroad-in-the-Landscape," p. 203.
63. Marx, "The Railroad-in-the-Landscape," p. 203.
64. Marx, "The Railroad-in-the-Landscape," p. 204.
65. Terrance Hawkes analyses well Umberto Eco's theories of ambiguity in the aesthetic uses of language. I believe Eco's theoretical framework of ambiguity in the particular use of (aesthetic) signifiers can easily and effectively be transported to the study of ambiguity in art. See Hawkes's *Structuralism and Semiotics* (Berkeley: University of California Press, 1977), p. 141.
66. Hawkes, *Structuralism and Semiotics*, p. 142.

Bibliography

Bloom, Harold. A Map of Misreading. New York: Oxford, 1975.

Bloom, Harold. *Poetry and Repression*. New Haven: Yale, 1976.

Cikovsky Jr., Nicolai."George Inness' *The Lackawanna Valley*: 'Type of the Modern'. " *The Railroad in American Art*. Eds. Susan Danly and Leo Marx. Cambridge, Massachusetts: MIT Press, 1988.

Cikovsky, Jr., Nicolai, and Michael Quick. *George Inness*. Los Angeles: Los Angeles County Museum of Art, 1985.

Clark, Kenneth. *Landscape Into Art*. New York: Harper and Row, 1976.

Coates, Paul. *The Double and the Other*. New York: St. Martin's, 1988.

Cuddon, J.A. *A Dictionary of Literary Terms*. London: Andre Deutsch, 1977.

Emerson, Ralph Waldo. *Selected Essays*. New York: Penguin, 1982.

Foucault, Michel. *The Use of Pleasure: The History of Sexuality, Vol. 2*. New York: Vintage, 1985.

Freud, Sigmund. *On Metapsychology*. New York: Pelican, 1977.

Freud, Sigmund. *The Interpretation of Dreams*. New York: Pelican, 1976.

Hawkes, Terence. *Structuralism and Semiotics*. Berkeley: University of California Press, 1977.

Kasson, John F. *Civilizing the Machine*. New York: Grossman Publishers, 1976.

Klein, Melanie. *Love, Guilt and Reparation*. London: Hogarth Press, 1977.

Lemaire, Anika. *Jacques Lacan*. New York: Routledge, 1977.

Maddox, Kenneth W. "Asher B.Durand's *Progress*: The Advance of Civilization and the Vanishing American." *The Railroad in American Art*. Eds. Susan Danly and Leo Marx. Cambridge: MIT Press, 1988.

Marx, Leo. "The Railroad in the Landscape." *The Railroad in American Art. Eds. Susan Danly and Leo Marx. Cambridge: MIT Press, 1988.*

Marx, Leo. *The Machine in the Garden: Technology and the Pastoral Ideal in America*. London: Oxford University Press, 1964.

Novak, Barbara. *Nature and Culture: American landscape and Painting*. New York: Oxford University Press, 1980.

Norris, Christopher. *Deconstruction: Theory and Practice*. London: Methuen, 1982.

Schivelbusch, Wolfgang. *The Railway Journey: Trains and Travel in Nineteenth Century*. New York: Urizen Books, 1979.

Taylor, G.R. *The Transportation Revolution: 1815 - 1860*. New York: Rinehart, 1951.

Wright, Elizabeth. *Psychoanalytic Criticism: Theory in Practice*. London: Methuen, 1984.

Relational Chaos and Residue: Wallace Stevens' *Madame la Fleurie*

4

Nothing separates one pole from the other, the initial from the terminal: there is just a sort of contraction into each other, a fantastic telescoping, a collapsing of the two traditional poles into one another: an IMPLOSION—an absorption of the radiating model of causality, of the differential mode of determination, with its positive and negative electricity—'an implosion of meaning.'

—Jean Baudrillard, *Simulations*

It is only proper to ask how such terms as relational chaos and residue apply to *Madame La Fleurie*. Both terms define an alternative process of reading *Madame la Fleurie*. Relational chaos and residue are interdependent functions of the same mechanism: the former is the causal generator of its effect, residue. It will be argued that the residual effect of relational chaos in *Madame la Fleurie* produces a state of indeterminacy in the reading process. The equation relational chaos plus residue equals indeterminacy is not only valid for *Madame la Fleurie*—although *Madame la Fleurie* will be the only poetic object of study in the present essay—but is valid as a model of reading for most of Wallace Stevens' poetry.[1] Relational chaos will be defined as the relational play of violent difference, such as, for example, the play between the present and past tense without logical reason, or the play between radically opposed senses. Residue is the stain that is left after such interplay is over: indeterminacy is the doubt that residue produces in relation to sense.[2] The aim of this essay will be to chart—and to some degree interpret (it is at this stage in the reading process that indeterminacy enters)—relational chaos and residue in *Madame la Fleurie*. The structure of the present study will have two parts. Part one will examine Claudia Yukman's arguments in "An American Poet's Idea of Language."[3] Part two will be an application of Yukman's arguments and my own in an analysis of the text under study.

Yukman, in "An American Poet's Idea of Language" begins by stating that Stevens' language anticipates a deconstructionist and postmodernist idea of language. Her concern after such an original moment of disclosure[4] is to reveal evidence of what is American and postmodern or deconstructive[5] in Stevens' use of language. The factor which distinguishes Stevens and Whitman from earlier English predecessors, for Yukman, is the use of syntactic parallelism as poetic device:

> Because syntactic parallelism is not the established structural principle in English-language poetry that it is, for example, in Hebrew poetry, this aspect of both Whitman's and Stevens' poetics—which connects them and which may distinguish an American way of thinking about language from both English and continental language theories—has not been seen as critically relevant.[6]

Emphasis on the analysis of syntactic parallelism in Stevens' poetry is also of critical relevance in relation to the deconstructive element. A text-specific study of a great number of Stevens' poems with emphasis on syntactic parallelism consistently reveals a textual deconstructing process—a relational chaos and residue at work in the poetry. To illustrate this process, a definition of syntactic parallelism and its consequent relation to Jean Baudrillard's theory of equivalence and implosion is required.

In Chris Baldick's *The Concise Oxford Dictionary of Literary Terms* parallelism is defined as: the arrangement of similarly constructed clauses, sentences, or verse lines in a pairing or other sequence suggesting some correspondence between them. The effect of parallelism is usually one of balanced arrangement achieved through repetition of the same syntactic forms. Where the elements arranged in parallel are sharply opposed, the effect is one of antithesis.[7] The structure of Stevens' *Madame la Fleurie* is clearly one of syntactic parallelism which, according to Yukman, suggests equivalence between the separate and antithetical parts.[8] This equivalence inherent in syntactic parallelism is of interest when examined in combination with Baudrillard's theory of equivalence in *Simulations*.

Baudrillard's physics' of the social mirror and define Stevens' use of structure and language in *Madame la Fleurie*. The opening quotation to this essay describes the condition of the postmodern social: an equivalence exists among objects and subjects—hierarchy, order, and cause and effect are lost in a meaningless implosion. Such a social is always already in a meaning gap where indeterminacy is less a product of molecular randomness than a product of the abolition, pure and simple, of the relation.[9] Although the opening quotation is descriptive of the effect of Stevens' use of language and structure, the latter one, on indeterminacy, is not, because randomness and relation are indeed representative qualities in Stevens' work. It is for this reason that the term deconstruction applies more readily to Stevens than the term postmodernism. (A postmodern work is beyond relation; whereas a deconstructive work—functioning always in the mode of most of Stevens' poems—is primarily concerned with the gaps, blindspots, weaknesses, and relational aspects of language.) The use of syntactic parallelism as structure, in Yukman's view, is the generating cause of relation in Stevens' use of language.[10]

As a structure, syntactic parallelism, implies that reading should occur in the midst of the relation of the separate parts. A vital question to ask at this point is what occurs to relation first and reading afterwards when, as Yukman notes, a loss of boundaries exists between the antithetical syntactic units.[11] Relation in such a language context is random, arbitrary, chaotic, and open in quality; reading and sense are generated within the relational play of chaotic equivalence. Baudrillard's theory of implosion describes the inwardness—inside rather than outside—of Stevens' use of language and structure. Reading, in Stevens, therefore, occurs within an inward relational chaos, that is always language based, which forcibly produces residue at the level of sense. Unlike Baudrillard's social indeterminacy, Stevens' linguistic indeterminacy[12]—an effect of residue—is dependent on the random relational play of its conflicting parts.[13]

Another question must be asked at this stage: what are the effects of random relational play of language on context, language, and criticism? Stevens' use of language and its relation to context is too general a topic to be discussed reductively.[14] It is however possible and appropriate to this study to examine context in the relational-chaotic poem. (Stevens' *Madame la Fleurie*, albeit a weak example, is an example of the mode in question. A good example of a strong relational-chaotic poem is Stevens' *Les Plus Belles Pages*.) The contexts of relational-chaotic poems are language determined contexts—not language contexts created through effective use of communication, but, instead, created through a conflicting relational play of language and structure. Such contexts bear little connection to an hors texte', to an otherness—a quality in a physical social for instance—which escapes sense, in the manner of a residual effect, and exists outside the text of language.[15] Ironically enough, the contexts of relational-chaotic poems also achieve an otherness' in the form of a residual effect: in this instance however by remaining solely within the relational frameworks of language.

It suffices to argue that language contexts produced under a relational-chaotic model of language are foreign and abstract in nature. In relation to language and sense, the relational chaos model renders language strange. The conflicting relational use of language generates a wholly other sense of language as extra terrestrial—as overwhelmingly beyond human structure and control.[16] Such violent effects on context and language consequently effect,[17] according to Yukman, an open road between writer and reader. It is this open road between a relational-chaotic text and reader that makes criticism of the specific objects under consideration succumb to a plurality of theoretical positions and languages. Criticism of such texts becomes a form of chaotic writing: any synthesis of approaches or singular approach to the relational-chaotic poem, taken from a plurality of choice, is fruitful. A scientific realist approach and its idiomatic use of language is as valid as a deconstructive approach, or is as valid as both combined together, thus indicating the constitutional openness and arbitrariness of relational chaos in language. It is therefore possible to deduce that criticism in confrontation with such objects of study cannot logically be positive in nature: its only truth is that it is relative to the relational chaos it confronts and to the chaotic writing such poems have produced.

At this point it is necessary to ground some of the above mentioned theoretical concerns by analyzing Stevens' *Madame la Fleurie*. Of primary concern will be to see whether the relational chaos plus residue equals indeterminacy hypothesis applies to the poem in question. *Madame la Fleurie*, like many of Stevens' poems, has determinate qualities: parts of its overall structure can be contextualized. It is possible to place to a near positive degree, at times, the figures and objects of *Madame la Fleurie* (this mark makes it a weak relational-chaotic poem). When, however, the different parts of the whole are brought together—as they are in *Madame la Fleurie*—a relational exchange is born out of an interplay of radically antithetical elements. The effect of relational exchange on an almost positive context is that a residue inevitably develops, thus causing such a context to become foreign in nature.

A consequent and larger effect of relational exchange in *Madame la Fleurie* is general indeterminacy. (Stevens' poem is indeterminate only when the colliding parts are brought together in relational exchange through the equivalence effect of syntactic parallelism. Otherwise, it is possible to valorize one part over the others and consequently argue that *Madame la Fleurie* is a poem about death for example, as Mark Halliday has done in *Stevens and the Interpersonal*. It is vital to study the structure of relational exchange, which is itself the causal mechanism of indeterminacy of sense in *Madame la Fleurie*. The basic constitutional parts of the structure of relational exchange are imprecise use of language and illogical or random shifts in tense and subject matter. These marks problematize the act of reading and make it impossible to orient sense in a single direction—sense floats aimlessly between polarities—in *Madame la Fleurie*. It bears repeating that if the relational exchange of chaotic elements generates residue, which in turn produces indeterminacy, then the causal factor of relational exchange is the effect of equivalence produced through the use of syntactic parallelism as structure. This is to simply say that if verse pattern in *Madame la Fleurie* is indicative of equivalence between the parts, then an ensuing relational chaos exists when these separate (in sense only) yet equal parts are analyzed as a unity.[18] A vague sense may be produced when the chaotic relational activity reaches an end, but counterbalancing and causing such sense to be incomplete is the overpowering sense of residual indeterminacy. It now remains to prove concretely, that residual indeterminacy applies to Stevens' *Madame la Fleurie*.

One of the causes of the relational exchange of chaos in *Madame la Fleurie* is the title's arbitrary connection to the content of the poem. Madame la Fleurie, a French name, linguistically contradicts the use of English language in the remainder of the poem. Although Madame la Fleurie may signify, separately, in either French or English language contexts, a chaotic relation develops when both languages are used appositionally. It is nevertheless necessary to try to undress such a tittle and see whether it logically relates to the whole.[19] La Fleur translates to the flower in English, and in most contexts would signify a specific plant, either cultivated or not by human beings in a natural environment. Such a detail could be of relevance, but one would have to forget or subtract the final vowels (i.e.,) of la Fleurie in a moment of apocope. Stevens however chooses Madame la Fleurie and not Madame la Fleur, thus determining the title to a high degree: la Fleurie is simply one out of a multitude of French surnames.

If a link exists between the title and its body it is achieved through the word madame: the words her, 'mother', and 'bearded queen' which appear in two of the three sections of *Madame la Fleurie*, are forcibly sensible in relation to madame. But even at the seeming apogee of sense in *Madame la Fleurie* an anomaly surfaces: 'bearded queen' does not logically and innocently relate to 'madame'. It is at such threshold points that a violent play of difference begins, a consequence of which is sense in a state of impasse. (Too many chaotic possibilities arise at such points, thus placing a reader in a position of undecidability in relation to sense.) What is the queen or madame in the above example? Is she a woman, a queen with an abnormal physiological condition? Or is madame a person who is half man/half woman: the androgyne? Several other creative possibilities exist, but the above are enough to indicate that even at the level of logic the connection between the title and its body is arbitrary and chaotic.[20]

The most significant cause of relational chaos in *Madame la Fleurie* is the collision of two plausible senses. The description of the male figure of *Madame la Fleurie* is the generating cause of duality of sense and subsequent collision. Sense A would have the male figure as foreigner from a weightless context, whereas sense B would have him as mortal who is about to be devoured. The interplay of senses, as can be imagined, is chaotic: context

A is otherworldly and therefore foreign; whereas, context B is earthly and therefore familiar. As will be illustrated in the following pages, the collision of sense A with sense B effects a relational-chaotic play of language and consequently of sense more generally.

Even within sense A the metaphor of the poem's protagonist is indeterminate: he may be read as either a Christ figure or extra-terrestrial. (But this is as close to determinate sense as one gets in both figures uncannily related through the effect of their supposed otherworldly contexts.) An examination of the initial sentence, 'Weight him down, O side-stars, with the great weightings of the end'[21] will help contextualize the space and sense of the first of two possible readings.[22]

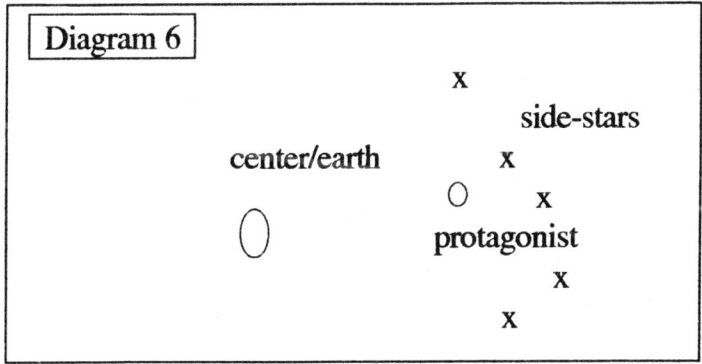

If the earth is the center, as is inferred in sentence three of the poem, 'Now he brings all that he saw into the earth' (CP507), then 'weight him down' and 'side-stars' invariably situates the male protagonist at a distance from the center, in an other than earthly context. Although 'weight him down' and 'side-stars' innocently locate an other worldliness, the signifier 'end' in the initial sentence, especially in connection with 'great', begins to effect a religious residue. (A second guessing game occurs at the level of interpretation: is 'he' simply an alien who must be 'grounded', or is he a religious figure who must return once more?)

The religious residue is determined when the signifier-doubles weight/wait engage in playful interaction. While wait, the obverse double of weight, does not appear in the text, the singular double of the plural 'weightings', waiting, appears shortly after and in the same section as sentence one in the form of the waiting parent; thus justifying and encouraging discourse on the play of the various forms of weightings/waiting. All play between weight/wait taken into consideration, the reader is literally left with an indefinite waiting parent'. (Indefinite because she may be either of three parents: a simple mother, the Virgin Mary, both of these playing a vital role in Sense A, or mother-earth.) Who is the indefinite parent waiting for and why? She (her sex having been determined in the poem) is waiting for him, 'Now, he brings all that he saw into the earth, to the waiting parent'(CP507).

The most determinate answer to why she waits for him are the devouring metaphors: 'His crisp knowledge is devoured by her, beneath a dew' and 'His grief is that his mother should feed on him, himself and what he saw' (CP507). But the devouring rationale for the cause of her waiting contradicts rather than supports both tracks (Track 1: protagonist as extra-terrestrial; Track 2: protagonist as Christ-figure) of Sense A. For Sense A to work, then, why she is waiting must remain indeterminate. Within the religious residue of Track 2, the narrative of his arrival 'into the earth', 'into' not necessarily signifying inside the soil in the linguistic context of section one and the parent's waiting, may be read as a condensed and warped revision of the immaculate conception. If one were to neglect the Virgin Mary metaphor and replace it with the simple mother metaphor but still remain within a religious framework, then her waiting could refer to 'His' second coming. Track 1 in Sense A, protagonist as extra-terrestrial in contrast, is arbitrary in relation to the indefinite parent's waiting and is, therefore, the least logical line of sense.

It now remains to see which other available schemata, of appropriate value to the present approach, either reinforce or contradict both tracks of Sense A. Placed at the beginning of sentence four, section one, His crisp knowledge' is most meaningful within the logical constraints of Track 2. In Revelation 22:13, John the Evangelist repeats the words of Christ: 'I am alpha and omega, the beginning and the end, the first and the last'.[23] According to the Bible, knowledge, especially of a 'crisp' variety, is always already enclosed in the Holy Trinity of Jesus-God-Holy Spirit. But even without the Bible as reference point, an exploration of the history of ideas and science indicates that humans have, at best experienced only fleeting moments of knowledge. If humans do not possess crisp knowledge, this is indicative in the incessant shifts of paradigms of knowlege in history, then the above trope is best suited to the Christ reading, and potentially to the extraterrestrial reading, of the protagonist in Sense A.

Finally, the trope of language as foreign entity to the protagonist, 'It was a language he spoke, because he must, yet did not know', contradicts Track 2 but accurately compliments Track 1. Language cannot be construed as foreign within the belief system of religious text and context, and specifically in relation to a Christ figure because, as John the Baptist proclaims in Chapter 1:1 of his own verse: 'In the beginning was the Word, and the Word was with God, and the Word was God'.[24]

An exciting paradox has been reached in Sense A: at a simple level of sense a Christ-figure is an extra-terrestrial (he, in whatever form, is not simply of the profane earth) but, at a more complex level of signification, and specifically in relation to the issue of language, a violent difference separates a Christ-figure, who it would seem is naturally aware of his father's words, from an alien who would not be a naturally determined speaking subject of an either religious or human construct. The issue of language's otherness in connection to the protagonist of *Madame la Fleurie* clearly reinforces Track 1 of Sense A, but radically opposes Track 2.[25]

The second plausible reading of *Madame la Fleurie* is that of a mortal about to be devoured by the metaphorical use of the earth as mother. This reading, in antithesis to Sense A which is most determinate in section one, reaches peak determination in section three. The other remaining section, two, may be read, always under the constraints of the present framework, as either a transcription of elision or as the battleground of sense, of both senses, in *Madame la Fleurie*. Residual determination of Sense B, protagonist as mortal to be devoured, is, like its double is, (Sense A), arrived at in the initial sentence of the poem, a mark which determines in a strong manner the ultimate indeterminacy of *Madame la Fleurie*.[26] If one omits 'side-stars' from the first sentence, then 'weight him down' and 'end' can be read, alternatively to Sense A, as a bringing to an end the course of existence of the protagonist. An almost literal reading of line three of section one, 'Now, he brings all that he saw into the earth, to the waiting parent' (CP507), suggests another form of bringing: this time of past experience (saw) into the present presence (now, brings) of the soil/grave.

The last sentence of section two, 'It was a page he had found in the handbook of heartbreak'(CP507), also supports determination of Sense B. The use of the past perfect tense (he had found) in relation to language,[27] it is language that he finds in the handbook of heartbreak, stabilizes the protagonist's discourse in two ways: first, the consciousness necessary to speaking a language is situated in the distant past and second, a logical consequence of the first is that the protagonist is now placed within the constraints of a context which does not permit interactive communication. Such a context is, logically, a grave, in which language and communication become past perfect in sense when confronted with the absence of physical presence. (The consistent interplay of the simple past, past perfect, and present tense within the opaque semi-narrative of *Madame la Fleurie* is indeed symptomatic of a 'once having lived' and a present mortality.)

The use of the word 'heartbreak' seems to fortify and becomes most determinable in relation to the theme of the protagonist as human being in Sense B. Although 'heartbreak' may be a meaningful concept in religious textuality, such as in the example of the prophet Simeon telling the Virgin Mary that her newborn son will be a 'sword in thy heart', it is for the most part an emotional structure representative of simple subjects of the earth.[28] The apogee of Sense B is reached in section three of *Madame la Fleurie*, and especially in sentences one, 'The black fugatos are strumming the blacknesses of black', and part of four, 'His grief is that his mother should feed on him, himself and/what he saw,/in that distant chamber, a bearded queen, wicked in her dead/light'(CP507). (It is of interest to observe that, except for two examples, the other three examples which function as support for Sense

B are the same examples used for Sense A in the present reading of *Madame la Fleurie*. This doubling technique used for opposed senses in *Madame la Fleurie* points to the undeniable free play of language in the examples.)

The repetition of black, its pervasive trace in section three, clearly settles the possibility of a funeral context. The sentence which immediately follows, 'The thick strings stutter the finial gutturals'(CP507), determines sense and context to an even greater degree: the protagonist, who is now dead, is experiencing the final sounds, vocal and instrumental, of his funeral. ('Finial' not only doubles final, to a near degree, phonetically, but is also semantically related: an ornament *finishing* off the apex of a roof, pediment, gable, tower-corner, canopy, etc.'[29] Although the first part of the last sentence of *Madame la Fleurie* assists Sense B's thematic structure it annotates the protagonist's grief that his mother, earth, should feed on all aspects, objective (him) and subjective (himself), of his past experience (saw) the latter part effects a residue which underdetermines, interminably, section three and the poem more generally.[30] The word 'distant' effects an endless dissemination of sense: is that distant chamber' located in the earth as the grave is, but only much further away, or is the 'bearded queen' suddenly situated amongst the sleepiness of the 'moon' and 'side-stars' (a context once already inhabited by the protagonist).

Two loosely constructed senses, which are in themselves not full proof, arise out of the language of *Madame la Fleurie* (thus potentially indicating the relational or oppositional grammar of language more generally). Some critics have argued in defense of Sense B, and it is fair to claim that Sense B is a little stronger than Sense A, but to omit Sense A and the problems it generates altogether is symptomatic of a quick and misguided reading. What has been claimed, implicitly, thus far is that *Madame la Fleurie* is a complex text: Sense A disseminates in two different directions, the protagonist as either extra-terrestrial or Christ figure; and strong determination of Sense B explodes, causing endless dissemination and implosion of sense, when one reaches the final syntactic part of its favoured section (three). It is therefore possible to propose a logical deduction, determined by the conditions of *Madame la Fleurie*, at this point: neither the figures nor the context of the poem can be fully stabilized.

A consequence of such instability is that figures, contexts, tropes, and more generally sense in *Madame la Fleurie* cannot be reduced to simple statements such as Joseph Carrol's 'timeless mother'[31] or Mark Halliday's 'death poem'.[32] Neither does commentary such as Elizabeth Cook's on Madame la Fleurie come to appreciate its ultimate complexity and opacity:

Among other old subjects, we might note the late form of Florida as Madame la Fleurie, a wicked fairytale earth mother whose reality awaits us all. 'Venus has mostly vanished, though there is a mother with vague severed arms' (CP 438). As a force, she has become Penelope, the longed-for and longing woman of this earth. As with old subjects and arguments, so with old 'topoi'.[33]

Madame la Fleurie is all of the above and much more or less: it is probably best understood as an endless intertext in which seemingly contradictory qualities and codes are brought together in an endless relational-chaotic play of language. Thus the poem is, as Claudia Yukman would have it, an 'open road': no one can claim to have, and especially not the present writer, secret or determinate understanding of *Madame la Fleurie*. If there is a constant in *Madame la Fleurie* it would have to be the use of language in a complex, opaque, and radically duplicitous manner. According to the present examination of this 'open road', the sense produced of language as opaque and duplicitous finds causal generation in the relational play of antithetical structures.

The chaotic relational play of language and the after effect of residue which such play produces withdraws its potential reader into a state of undecidability in respect to its possible sense. Undecidability in the present analysis is reached when a logical and justifiable decision made between Sense A or Sense B is unjustifiable and impossible. The collision of senses further conditions a groundlessness which, once more, does not authorize, or does not provide space for final solutions to its mystery. Since there seems to be only residual, and therefore indeterminate, sense in *Madame la Fleurie*, a residual reading seems only possible, one which ideally competes, democratically, with all other residual readings of the text.

Notes

1. Other strong paradigms of relational-chaotic indeterminacy poems in Stevens are *The Emperor of Ice-Cream* and *Mozart, 1935*.

2. Indeterminacy therefore is a decision reached at the very end of the interpretive process. The decision to call a literary work indeterminate has obviously to do with how residue works against closure in a given text. It is subsequently fair to conclude that the very precondition of indeterminacy is the existence of residual sense in a text.

On the decision making process involved in defining a text as indeterminate see much of Jonathan Culler's work on critical theory. Culler is the critic who argued that a work is indeterminate when one reaches a juncture in the interpretive process where it is 'impossible' or 'unjustifiable' to decide on the meaning of the work. For different definitions of indeterminacy see also J. Hillis Miller (Stevens' Rock and Criticism as Cure, II) who insists that indeterminacy is a condition in texts which promotes an 'uncomfortable feeling' and the sense that something is 'missing' in the reading process; and Paul De Man (Semiology and Rhetoric) who intelligently argues that indeterminacy is the effect of a structural grammar which does not permit univocal sense.

3. Yukman's essay in *Critical Essays on Wallace Stevens*, eds. Steven Gould Axelrod and Helen Deese (Boston: G.K. Hall. 1988).

4. The irony and pun of original and disclosure is intended.

5. Yukman, "An American Poet's Idea of Language," 230, 231, 232.

6. Yukman, "An American Poet's Idea of Language," 231.

7. Baldick, *The Concise Oxford Dictionary of Literary Terms* (Oxford: Oxford UP, 1990), 160.

8. A syntactic parallelism structure also suggests correspondence between the parts. Such a structure creates a complex code when the parts are antithetical as in the case of *Madame la Fleurie*. Yukman, "An American Poets Idea of Language," 234, 236.

9. Jean Baudrillard, *Simulations*, trans. Paul Foss, Paul Patton, and Philip Beitchman (New York: Semiotext(e), 1983), 57.

10. Yukman, "An American Poet's Idea of Language," 236, 242.

11. Yukman does not answer the specific question, but she is quick to point out what the effects of a loss of boundaries produce in a poem of antithetical parts. Yukman writes the following about "Domination of Black," which is considered a paradigmatic poem of relational-antithetical play:

One of the obvious things to say of a poem like this—representative of so many of Stevens' texts in the problems for interpretation it stages—is that it is difficult if not impossible to contextualize the images. What room, what event, what meaning can the poem be seen to delimit except language itself? Like a riddle, "Domination of Black" reveals only rhetorically, as if it were telling us about something. Unlike a riddle, "Domination of Black" has no correct answer to be deciphered in puns. The more appropriate analogy in fact, given the poetics that generate this poem, would be prophetic or parabolic modes of discourse as they exist alongside a syntactical poetics in the Bible. Language goes strange, as does the language of Isaiah or Christ, in order to manifest an other-than-human reality. But as might be said of the biblical story of a God who writes and becomes the incarnate word, Stevens' poem is actually the ultimate human reality: language itself.

In sum, the primary feature of such poetry is language itself. When language is placed before narrative causality, as in the example of "Domination of Black," then interpretations of such poems tend to be open-ended. "An American Poets Idea of Language," 238.

12. According to some theorists the connection between the social and language is an invisible one. Language creates the social and vice-versa. Both are thought to be interdependent and sometimes unnecessarily confused as being the same object (see theorists like Derrida and Lacan who had at times believed that language is the generating factor of the social). Such approaches to explaining the social or language are always too reductive in nature. It is best to differentiate: the social is what it is (regardless of whether language is one of its components), and the same applies to language. This does not imply however that one system cannot at times influence the other.

Stevens is often seen to make the mistake of believing he can describe creatively reality processes—social or otherwise—in language. His poetry often takes for granted that an invisible thread exists between the two distinct systems. It is unfair however to argue that Stevens systematically falls into such a trap; some of his poems are well aware of the crucial differences between language and the social.

See Robert Erwin "The Great Language Panic," *The Antioch Review*, 45:4 (1987), 421-434, for an interesting but flawed discussion of how language influences the social. See also M.A.K. Halliday's "Language as Social Semiotic: the Social Interpretation of Language and Meaning," in *The Communication Theory Reader*, ed. Paul Cobley (London: Routledge, 1996), 88-93, in which social reality is defined as follows: "A social reality (or a culture) is itself an edifice of meanings, a semiotic construct. In this perspective, language is one of the semiotic systems that constitute a culture; one that is distinctive in that it serves as an encoding system for many (though not all) of the others." Halliday's thesis on the language-social relation is one of the most mature in contemporary linguistic theory.

13. It is better not to think that random codes of linguistic representation are chosen for a poem. Instead Stevens was consciously aware that the conflicting codes used in many of his indeterminate

poems would cause a random-relational play of words, phrases, and sentences. Therefore random is not used in the sense of unconsciously chosen structures of representation, but in the sense of random codes consciously brought together in order to achieve a specific effect.

14. Not all of Stevens' poems are random-relational in mode. *Anecdote of the Jar* and *Valley Candle* for instance do not represent conflicting codes of expression and therefore allow for a stable enough picture of context (wilderness in *Anecdote* and a valley in *Candle*). Consequently, it is vital to make clear that there is no single image of setting in Stevens' poetry; instead the context of Stevens' poetry is always shifting depending on whether a given poem is determinate or indeterminate.

15. It is necessary to discuss Simple R and Complex R. Simple Reality refers to a more or less describable physical setting or action. Although there is difference between an actual event and its linguistic description, it is more or less possible to describe accurately enough the step by step process of constructing a model airplane, or of heart surgery in a hospital. Some forms of the physical world are not as easily described or understood and therefore remain (temporarily or permanently) foreign to human language and consciousness. These forms can be interpreted as instances of Complex Reality. Everyone is aware of such moments in experience: at one point or another one has come across events or objects in the physical world that are momentarily foreign to previous conscious experience. It is during such instances that language fails and cannot fully describe, or describe at all, what has been experienced.

In sum Simple R refers to what humans know of the world and experience, whereas Complex R refers to that factor in experience which residually escapes knowledge, and is, at least initially, abstract and foreign in nature. Complex R does not simply relate to an external reality only, sometimes a known outer world can become complex due to internal factors.

16. The obvious contradiction here is that Wallace Stevens was very much in control of his language and structure. If Stevens' language gives the impression of being beyond human knowledge, it is due to the latter's crafty manipulation of codes, words, and phrases. Moreover Stevens was a living subject during a specific historical period (1879-1955), which implies that his use of language was necessarily both a condition (created by) and a conditioning factor (creative) of the time period. It is therefore wise to think of 'otherworldly' and 'beyond' as metaphors only in relation to language use.

17. It is not wrong to interpret some of Wallace Stevens' poetry—especially of the relational-chaotic variety—as the poetry of endless effects.

18. Imagine a precise structure of equivalent parts that are for the most part unrelated to each other. What would be the effect of such a structure? Obviously a sense of relational-chaos would ensue the

reading of such a unit, since all the parts (sentences or phrases) are equal to each other structurally, but separate to each other thematically.

Madame la Fleurie cannot be read in parts if one desires univocal sense of the poem. One part may have a sense wholly logical and meaningful to itself, but completely contradictory to another part of the same poem. Since poems should be read as complete units, the only rational sense of Madame la Fleurie a critic can arrive at is that it is indeterminate.

19. All puns are once again intended.

20. At this point it is necessary to state that a blindspot may exist in the essay in relation to who Madame la Fleurie was historically or otherwise, if she/he was at all a historical or legendary figure. Nevertheless, knowledge of who Madame la Fleurie was would not alter the present interpretation of the poem, it would only make it more complete.

21. From this point on quotations from *Madame la Fleurie* will be followed by (CP 507) in the essay. CP refers to Stevens' *The Collected Poems*.

22. Two strong interpretations, leading in different directions, are possible. It is this condition of two polarities (A and Z) that functions as another structural effect which is creative of the poem's indeterminacy. When interpretation A differs from interpretation Z, and both are equally valid, an open space of indeterminacy is created between both points.

Diagram:

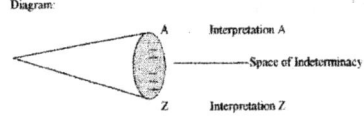

23. *The Holy Bible*, (Revelation), King James Version, (New York: Ivy Books, 1991), 1112.

24. *The Holy Bible*, (John), 940.

25. The otherness of language, or its other worldly quality, is an issue many have commented upon, including Jacques Lacan and Paul De Man (in psychoanalytic theory, critical theory) and Laurie Anderson (in music).

26. *Madame la Fleurie* is not only indeterminate as a complete unit, but also in its parts. Some of its individual parts (i.e., 'Weight him down, O side stars, with the great weightings of the end.') are indeterminate in themselves. Such indeterminate units add to the overall indeterminacy of the greater unit.

27. Except for section three, *Madame la Fleurie* is grammatically structured by the use of past tenses (simple past and past perfect). Here are some of the verb forms used in the poem: looked, lived,

saw, was, told, spoke, did, and had found. This grammatical effect supports the interpretive analysis of Sense B, of protagonist as mortal who is no longer part of the living world.

28. 'Heartbreak' is indeed a concept very much representative of specific forms of human experience. As has been pointed out in the essay, however, it also leaves an inevitable religious trace behind. The Bible is, after all, a narrative of heartbreak. It is over this word and concept, then, that one of the battles of sense transpires since heartbreak signifies equally well in both simple human context and religious experience.

29. Knowing Stevens' fascination with word-play, it is fair to substitute finial' with final, especially since the linguistic context in which finial appears (end, blacknesses of black, dead) lures one to do so. For a good analysis of word-play generally in Stevens see Eleanor Cook's *Poetry, Word-Play, and Word-War in Wallace Stevens* (Princeton: Princeton UP, 1988).

The definition of finial is to be found in *The Concise Oxford Dictionary*, ed. R.E. Allen, (Oxford: Oxford UP, 1990), 439.

30. Mary Doyle Springer has written an intelligent essay from a relativistic perspective on the indefinite endings of Stevens' poems, "Closure in a Half Light: Wallace Stevens' Endings'," *The Wallace Stevens Journal*, 16 : 2 (1992). She does not however analyze indefinite endings to sentences in the poems under scrutiny. As *Madame la Fleurie* reveals, what is true of the poem as a whole, is also true of some of its smaller parts. The last two lines of the poem have an indefinite end to them, which is indicative of anti-closure at both the macro and micro level. It is therefore possible to deduce—since there are other indefinite endings to smaller units—that *Madame la Fleurie* has an indefinite ending, but that it is also composed of a plurality of micro indefinite endings at the level of sentences or phrases.

31. See Joseph Carrol's, *Wallace Stevens' Supreme Fiction: A New Romanticism* (Baton Rouge: Louisiana State University Press, 1987), 146.

32. See Mark Halliday's *Stevens and the Interpersonal* (Princeton: Princeton University Press, 1991), 109, for a reading of *The Owl in the Sarcophagus* and *Madame la Fleurie* as death poems that have a special relation to a reader.

33. See Eleanor Cook's *Poetry, Word-Play and Word-War in Stevens* (Princeton: Princeton University Press, 1988), 301.

Bibliography

1. On Wallace Stevens

Altieri, Charles. "Wallace Stevens' Metaphors of Metaphor: Poetry as Theory." *American Poetry* 1:1 (1983) Fall: 27-48.

Arensberg, Mary. " 'Golden Vacancies': Wallace Stevens' Problematics of Place and Presence." *The Wallace Stevens Journal* 10:1 (1986) Spring.

Argyros, Alex. "The Residual Difference: Wallace Stevens and American Deconstruction." *New Orleans Review* 13:1 (1986) Spring: 20-31.

Axelrod, Steven Gould, and Helen Deese (eds.). *Critical Essays on Wallace Stevens*. Boston: G.K. Hall, 1988.

Beehler, Michael. T.S. Eliot, *Wallace Stevens, and the Discourses of Difference*. Baton Rouge: Louisiana State University Press, 1987.

Bloom, Harold. *Wallace Stevens: The Poems of Our Climate*. Ithaca: Cornell University Press, 1976.

Brogan, Jacqueline. *Stevens and Simile: A Theory of Language*. Princeton, New Jersey: Princeton University Press, 1986.

Cook, Eleanor. "Directions in Reading Wallace Stevens: Up, Down, Across." *Lyric Poetry: Beyond New Criticism*. Eds. Chavia Hosek and Patricia Parker. Ithaca: Cornell University Press, 1985.

"Wallace Stevens and the King James Bible." *Essays in Criticism* 41:3 (1991) July: 240-252.

Gelpi, Albert (ed.). *Wallace Stevens: The Poetics of Modernism*. Cambridge: Cambridge University Press, 1985.

Halliday, Mark. *Stevens and the interpersonal*. Princeton, New Jersey: Princeton University Press, 1991.

Hoffman, N.M. "The Caesura in the Poetry of Wallace Stevens." *The Wallace Stevens Journal* 15:2 (1991) Fall: 144-164.

Kang, Du-Hyoung. "Stasis versus Continuity: Mallarme and Wallace Stevens." *The Wallace Stevens Journal* 13:1 (1989) Spring: 38-52.

Leggett, B.J. *Wallace Stevens and Poetic Theory: Conceiving the Supreme Fiction*. Chapel Hill: University of North Carolina Press, 1987.

Leonard, J.S., and C.E. Wharton. *The Fluent Mundo: Wallace Stevens and the Structure of Poetry*. Athens, Georgia: University of Georgia Press, 1990.

Looze, Laurence N. de. "Poem as Process: Wallace Stevens' 'Metamorphosis'." *The Wallace Stevens Journal* 8:1 (1984) Spring: 18-21.

Parker, Patricia A. "The Motive for Metaphor: Stevens and Derrida." *Wiener Slavistisches Jahrbuch* 7:3-4 (1983) Fall: 76-88.

Perlis, Alan. *Wallace Stevens: A World of Transforming Shapes*. Lewisburg: Bucknell University Press, 1976.

Pollard-Gott, Lucy. "Fractal Repetition Structures in the Poetry of Wallace Stevens." *Language and Style* 19:3 (1986) Summer: 233-249.

Rieke, Alison. *The Senses of Nonsense*. Iowa City: University of Iowa Press, 1992.

"Stevens' Armchair Travel: The Sound of the Foreign." *The Wallace Stevens Journal* 15:2 (1991) Fall: 165-177.

Schaum, Melita. *Wallace Stevens and the Critical Schools*. Tuscaloosa, Alabama: University of Alabama Press, 1988.

Scroggins, Mark. "A 'Sense of Duration': Wallace Stevens, Louis Zukofsky, and 'Language'." *Sagetrieb* 11:1-2 (1992) Spr.-Fall: 67-83.

Serio, John N. (ed.). "Stevens and Postmodern Criticism." *The Wallace Stevens Journal* 7:3-4 (1983) Fall.

Springer, Mary Doyle. "Closure in a Half Light: Wallace Stevens' Endings." *The Wallace Stevens Journal* 16:2 (1992) Fall: 161-181.

2. On Indeterminacy

Bahti, Timothy. "Ambiguity and Indeterminacy." *Comparative Literature* 38:3 (1986) Sum.: 209-223.

Erwin, Robert. "The Great Language Panic." *The Antioch Review* 45:4 (1987) Fall: 421-434.

Graff, Gerald. "Determinacy/Indeterminacy." *Critical Terms For Literary Study*. Eds. Franck Lentricchia and Thomas McLaughlin. Chicago: University of Chicago Press, 1990.

Hartman, Geoffrey H. "The State of the Art of Criticism." *The Future of Literary Theory*. Ed. Ralph Cohen. New York: Routledge, 1989. 86-101.

Hornstein, Norbert, "Grammar, Meaning, and Indeterminacy." *The Chomskyian Turn*. Ed. Asa Kasher. Cambridge: Blackwell, 1991. 104-121.

Iser, Wolfgang. "Talk like Whales: A Reply to Stanley Fish." *Diacritics* 11:3 (1981) Fall: 82-87.

King, Terrance. "The Problem of Indeterminacy in Stevens." *Bucknell Review* 31:2 (1988): 149-155.

Miall, David S. "The Indeterminacy of Literary Texts: The View from the Reader." *Journal of Literary Semantics* 17:3 (1988) Nov.: 155-171.

Perloff, Marjorie. *The Poetics of Indeterminacy: Rimbaud to Cage*. Evanston, IL: Northwestern University Press, 1993.

Rouse, Joseph. "Indeterminacy, Empirical Evidence, and Methodological Pluralism." *Synthese* 86:3 (1991) March: 443-465.

Stern, David. "Midrash and Indeterminacy." *Critical Inquiry* 15:1 (1988) Autumn: 132- 161.

has also published the following books of related interest

A Cure of the Mind, *by Theodore Sampson*
Aphra Behn, *by George Woodcock*
Balance: Art and Nature, *by John Grande*
Beyond O.J., *by Earl Ofari Hutchinson*
Beyond Boundaries, *by Barbara Noske*
Every Life Is a Story, *by Fred H. Knelman*
Fateful Triangle, *by Noam Chomsky*
Humerous Sceptic, *by N.Anthony Bonaparte*
Military in Greek Politics, *by Thanos Veremis*
Mind Abuse, *by Rose Dyson*
Murray Bookchin Reader, *by Janet Biehl and Murray Bookchin*
Odyssey of a Public Intellectual, *by Andrea T. Levy*
Oscar Wilde, *by George Woodcock*
Perspectives on Power, *by Noam Chomsky*
Peter Kropotkin, *by George Woodcock*
Rethinking Camelot, *by Noam Chomsky*
Russian Literature, *by Peter Kropotkin*
Writers and Politics, *by George Woodcock*
Women Pirates, *by Ulrike Klausmann, Marion Meinzerin, Gabriel Kuhn*
Zapata of Mexico, *by Peter Newell*

send for a free catalogue of all our titles
BLACK ROSE BOOKS
C.P. 1258, Succ. Place du Parc
Montréal, Québec
H3W 2R3 Canada

or visit our web site at: http://www.web.net/blackrosebooks

To order books in North America:
(phone) 1-800-565-9523 (fax) 1-800-221-9985
In Europe: (phone) 44-0181-986-4854 (fax) 44-0181-533-5821

Printed by the workers of
VEILLEUX IMPRESSION À DEMANDE INC.
Longueuil, Québec
for Black Rose Books Ltd.